The
FOOD
LIFE

ALSO BY STEVEN JENKINS

Cheese Primer

ecco

An Imprint of HarperCollins*Publishers*

The

FOOD LIFE

Inside the
WORLD OF FOOD
with the
GROCER EXTRAORDINAIRE
at
Fairway

Steven Jenkins with recipes by *Mitchel London*

Black-and-white photography by
Michelle Sims

Color photography by
Quentin Bacon

THE FOOD LIFE. Copyright © 2008 by Steven Jenkins. All rights reserved. Printed in the United States of America. No part of this book may be used or reproduced in any manner whatsoever without written permission except in the case of brief quotations embodied in critical articles and reviews. For information, address HarperCollins Publishers, 10 East 53rd Street, New York, NY 10022.

HarperCollins books may be purchased for educational, business, or sales promotional use. For information, please write: Special Markets Department, HarperCollins Publishers, 10 East 53rd Street, New York, NY 10022.

FIRST EDITION

Designed by Sunil Manchikanti

Library of Congress Cataloging-in-Publication Data is available upon request.

ISBN: 978-0-06-123168-1

08 09 10 11 12 ID/RRD 10 9 8 7 6 5 4 3 2 1

I dedicate this book to

Howie and Nita Glickberg,

to Harold and Miriam Seybert,

and to David and Dorothy Sneddon.

Acknowledgments

I must express my gratitude to a number of people for the help and inspiration they gave me for this book. Howard Glickberg, Harold Seybert, and David Sneddon first and foremost, for it was they who created Fairway, and it was they who gave me the opportunity to make Fairway my life's obsession.

Certainly my wife, Michelle Sims, belongs at the top here for her solid support of my long hours, working holidays, frequent moaning, and filthy, smelly work clothes, not to mention her glorious photography within.

My agent, Jane Dystel of Dystel & Goderich Literary Management, and my editors Daniel Halpern and Emily Takoudes at Ecco have been just wonderful. The efforts of Mary Goodbody, Ana Deboo, and Zoe Singer have proved crucial in the creation of this book.

I must also thank the following at Fairway for their many years of excellence and expertise: John Rossi, Paul Weiner, Peter Romano, Herb Ruetsch, Brian Riesenburger, and Ray Venezia are each the best in the industry at what they do.

My close friends in Europe who serve to grease the axle of commerce for me have been instrumental in keeping Fairway on the cutting edge of serious food—Georges Perrot in Nîmes; Isabelle Drouet in Lot-et-Garonne; Laurent Koubbi in Rennes; Peter and Tony DeMarco in Barcelona and Connecticut; Luigi, Maria, and Mario Sidoni in Milan; Heinz Muller in Paris; and Nicolas Medard, also in Paris.

Avanelle Rivera has been doing all the work that makes Fairway's cheese operations so successful, and seems not to mind that I take all the credit for it. Our general managers have the toughest jobs of all. James Flores, Joe Reda, Rick Garcia, and David Serrano—this Kölsch is for you.

Contents

Foreword

by Simon Schama

If it were possible (and it should be) to award the Congressional Medal of Honor to a food market, Fairway would already have been decorated for its service to appetite. For decades it's waged war against the tyranny of sterile, flavorless banality that is food shopping in supermarketland across the nation. But it's also the enemy of the precious. Fairway isn't for dainty nibbling; it's an intelligent gorger's heaven, a command to experience the relish of life and get the lost lusciousness back to the palate. Inside its doors are microworlds, each with its own distinctive savour and attitude—the in-your-face rawness of the meat department with customers bulked up in their chill-friendly quilted jackets; the cornucopic produce department where the organic section—against the orthodoxies of the age—is tolerated rather than sanctified. But for many of us, the heart of the whole damned thing is the cheese domain, presided over by Steven Jenkins, who in this fabulous book manages to reproduce exactly the kind of riotous relish that makes Fairway a perpetual springtime for the palate. Jenkins gets kvetchy over his pre-Fairway troubles with other retailers, less appreciative of the innocent abundance of his enthusiasm; he gets seriously hot and excited in his forays into European markets like Rungis outside Paris (if he had seen the original Les Halles it might have sent him over the edge). It's Jenkins we have to thank for the translation of Rabelaisian excess into a stationary New York festival of aroma, color, and texture.

Fairway is rightly famous for its delectable crankiness: actual human beings who can charm you; snap at you; make jokes (as lame as most of the ones featured on the neon billboard over the Henry Hudson Parkway); or on a cold winter's Friday night, chat you into cheeriness. Jenkins, who is himself a gloriously wild man in a grocery store, has richly multiple personalities, all on uninhibited display in the book. He can wax professorial when it comes to Agen prunes or get erotically out of control when it comes to cheese. Jenkins's ode to Vacherin is off limits to grade-schoolers.

In between the rich-dish essays are recipes from Mitchel London (what kind of New York name is *that*?), all of which display the full-on embrace of freshness, ripeness, richness, and succulent simplicity; a distaste for the overrefined (there's a terrific and dependable guide to cooking the perfect burger). This is a book that is all about shopping, cooking, and eating. You'll laugh a bit and drool a lot, and if you use the book as it should be used, its pages will be heavily, splendidly stained.

Introduction

I suppose people who have worked like dogs for a long time feel that everybody else is terribly interested in whatever it is they've been doing all these years, and that it is just natural for them to write about it. Surely everyone who reads this book will find it riveting. Now, that's silly, but it's true. People think their lives have been immensely worthwhile and worthy of note. Attention. Validation.

I've been working in a supermarket for more than thirty years. How cool is that? And I am convinced that you will find this account of my selfless sacrifice and peasantlike endeavors a source of endless fascination, brimming—nay, overflowing—with world-wise and -weary information that will make you wiser and worldlier in a lot less time than had you not chosen to read this. After all, if you're holding this book now, you are an aesthete. You are serious about food. You love it. You also love most, if not all, of your immediate family members, and you have love (or near love) for many people in your social circle. And it is crucial that you have enough food savvy to understand that what's important in this life is the food. The way I look at things, if you can't eat it, what's the point?

So we have established that you possess the requisite food savvy. Now we must concern ourselves with your food knowledge, which is completely different from savvy. Nothing else really matters.

Perhaps you're worried that you really know nothing about food. How could you know anything? You're not a food professional. All you do is eat it. That's not culinary scholarship—that's survival. Sure, eating is convivial and therefore *fun,* but you don't even know how to shop, much less cook. No need to panic. This is where I come in.

I know tons of stuff, but food is the thing I know the most about. And how did I learn so much? I taught myself. Some of the biggest food ignoramuses I've ever known were classically trained at highfalutin cooking schools. Those schools focus on the restaurant business, one my dad told me to never get involved in. On the basis of my experience in kitchens and with chefs and restaurant workers, I'm astonished and grateful that he was so right. Restaurants wouldn't have been for me. What I like to think about is, maybe, what to do with food. But also—Where does it come from? Which is the best, and why? Why is it, more or less, so significant? What is the most enjoyable way to serve it? What should it cost? What are the tricks of it, its quirks, and the proper seasons for it?

Learning about food by traveling to where it comes from and realizing the historical significance of it; talking to the people and animals responsible for it; looking up its origin on a map and knowing exactly where that is and having been there more than once; touching it, smelling it, looking at it, carrying it around with you—*that's* what I consider fun. It's the expertise I bring to Fairway and pass on to anyone who shops there in the spirit of wanting to *learn.*

You might think that if everyone lived near a Fairway Market, restaurants would suffer. But that's not necessarily true. All four Fairways are busy most of the time, but it looks as though restaurants in the same neighborhoods are, too; and more and more restaurants open every day. It's as if nobody wants to cook anymore. In fact, cooking at home has been in decline for the last ten years, so I have read. It didn't use to be this way. The early 1980s were a time of frenzy over home cooking. Dean & DeLuca was the result of Joel and Giorgio's wanting to create a store for cooks. So I'm thinking that maybe if people had ready access to all the foodstuffs we offer at Fairway, they'd feel less compelled to blow off cooking dinner and less inclined to go out and blow way too much money on food they're made to feel privileged to be allowed to order in the first place.

I suppose the truest testament to Fairway's place in the New York food world is the fact that so many chefs and caterers shop here.

But how can the home cook use Fairway? How can everyone take advantage of what Fairway offers? How should any shopper approach food marketing? And I don't mean just plopping things into a shopping cart. A good market makes culinary life worthwhile—and I've devoted myself to making Fairway the best of the best.

Let me tell you about it.

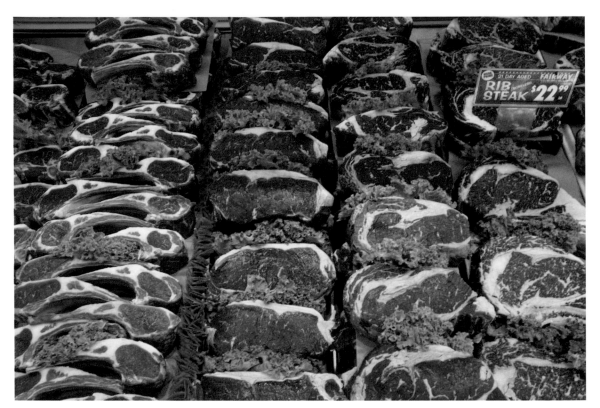

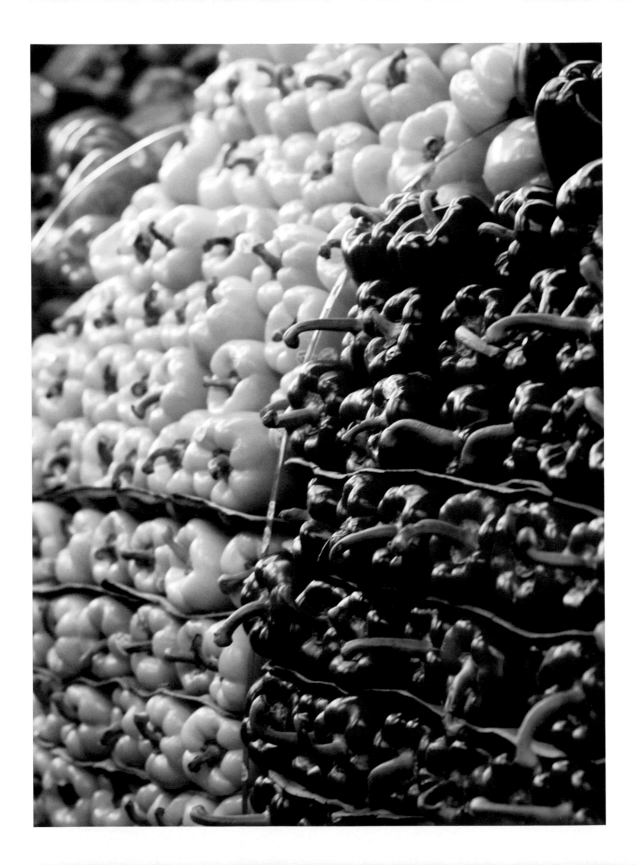

The
FOOD
LIFE

1

From Had It Up to Here to Having It All:

My Road to Fairway

It was late 1979. I had never even heard of Fairway Market. But I had had all I could take of Henry Lambert and Pasta & Cheese. After all, I'd been working at the cheese counter there for at least six months. Henry worked for Saul Steinberg, the infamous, pioneering corporate raider and conglomerate magnate who built the Reliance companies; Henry was CEO of his real estate–office building construction arm, Continental Cities. A born Upper East Sider, he was unmarried, wealthy, and smug, and he traveled all the time.

Henry was a workaholic, and in that spirit, his hobby during the late 1970s to mid-1980s was his three-store chain of pasta shops, the ones that offered fresh pasta to Upper East Siders. Raffetto's of Houston Street was the reigning producer of fresh pasta in New York, but it supplied only restaurants and sold from its storefront in its immediate neighborhood, South Greenwich Village and SoHo. Most East Siders might travel as far downtown as Houston Street to go to Dean & DeLuca at Broadway and Prince Street, the talk of the town since September 1977, but not for any other reason—and certainly not for fresh pasta. But with the advent of the Pasta & Cheese shops, fresh pasta was suddenly in vogue—as was traveling to Europe, and as was cheese. Henry's hobby, his shops, had recently been validated in print by the great Mimi Sheraton, the *New York Times*'s restaurant critic par excellence, whom I adore to this day, ever since she referred to her colleague and rival, the restaurant critic Gael Greene, as "Ben Franklin in a yachting cap." Mimi also validated me in print at around the same time, crediting me with having brought to New York and Pasta & Cheese the greatest cheeses in Italy, cheeses that had never been sold here at retail before—Fontina d'Aosta, *mozzarella di bufala,* mascarpone, robiolas such as Murazzano and Roccaverano, and the like.

I had gone to work for Henry shortly after I'd had it up to here with Giorgio DeLuca, cofounder and owner of Dean & DeLuca. I was Joel and Giorgio's first hire, and actually I adored them both—they were wonderful people. Joel died a couple of years ago. He was a terrific fellow, as is his partner Jack Ceglic, who deserves as much credit for Dean & DeLuca as do Joel and Giorgio. It's just that in those days I hated Giorgio's guts because he treated me like hired help. As if I weren't.

D&D was an earthshaking happening in our business, indeed in lots of businesses, changing everything. My contribution was creating the cheese operation there. Nowhere in the United States were French and Italian cheeses available in such variety; nor were they merchandised in this fashion—that is, taken out from behind the glass of refrigerators and refrigerated shelves and displayed dramatically in rows on a countertop. This was a French conceit that was revolutionary in our business. Designers, architects, artists, writers—all kinds of people who wanted to make their mark—were influenced by that and the other things we were doing with food at D&D.

A Little Holiday Cheer

Henry's brother Ben was a Wall Street banker and investor and, like Saul Steinberg, a familiar figure in the society columns. Ben had lots of friends, and that year, a few days before Christmas, Henry called me—at home, at night, at the last minute—and informed me that Ben needed a few dozen gift baskets put together and parcel-posted hither and yon to various boldface names all around the country. We didn't use FedEx or DHL in those days—we used just UPS—and nothing was easy. We had no fax machines, computers, or ATMs, of course. I was the go-to guy for this task, because I was the designated tastemaker for Pasta & Cheese. So I frantically loaded up thirty-six or so wicker baskets with what I thought were the most delicious and glorious foodstuffs in the universe, provender any self-respecting food sophisticate would kill for—wooden boxes of Vacherin Mont d'Or, a pudding-soft, stunningly delicious French cheese that is de rigueur at Christmastime in France and pretty much unheard of in New York City, along with softball-size, boneless spheres of string-wrapped, super-smoky Westphalian hams from the local hero Schaller & Weber; and a few other things, probably a Tuscan olive oil and a bottle of raspberry vinegar, both new stars on the nascent though growing "gourmet" food scene. Again, this was 1979. These choices were absolute rock and roll. I figured I had nailed it and would doubtless hear from Henry that Ben was thrilled with the response his largesse had evoked.

Quite the contrary. The boxes traveled without refrigeration or ice packs. As most of the swells opened their boxes from good old Ben, it seems they were enveloped in an effluvium of serious cheese, and the hams were so smoky, as is the nature of Westphalian ham, that the contents of the box smelled not only like roadkill but like burned roadkill. Many of Ben's addressees thought it was a practical joke. A few reportedly vomited directly and conveniently right into the box. What a waste of perfectly good, merely room-temperature food!

Chefs, cooks, caterers, and lovers of fine food were mesmerized and inspired. Eli Zabar was the cherished prodigal son of the Zabar family and brother to Saul and Stanley, from whom Eli diverged in a most dramatic fashion. Eli moved from the West Side to the other world, the East Side of Manhattan, and to this day caters to food lovers who don't think chicken salad for twenty-eight dollars a pound is even slightly exorbitant.

Anyway, once I'd started working at Pasta & Cheese, Henry Lambert would often call me at my apartment—at night, on my day off, whenever he wanted some answers. He made one call too many that winter of 1980, and I told him up his nose with a rubber hose. The initial euphoria of this mature confrontation wore off in a matter of hours, and finding myself unemployed yet again, I began to rethink my situation. The next day I managed to get him back on the phone, whereupon I asked him where we stood.

Henry said, "Well, I'm standing on the inside, and you're standing on the outside."

That's what you call "closure," though in 1979 it was referred to as "unnecessarily restating the obvious" or, perhaps, "You can't quit—you're fired." That made three jobs in four years. A dangerous pattern had emerged.

So there I was, yet again, an unemployed cheesemonger. I was not lacking in self-esteem, and my work ethic was fine. I just couldn't stand my bosses.

After six years in New York, I had barely a pot to cook in. I had given up looking for acting work in the summer of 1975 and gotten that first job in a cheese shop not because I felt a calling for cheese but because I needed a job. I'd just driven back to New York from Florida, where I had been hired to play the psychotic Teddy in Mark Medoff's great play *When You Comin' Back, Red Ryder?* at the University of Florida. There I met Michelle Sims, the love of my life to this day. She played what's-her-name, the prudish violin player whom I am required to ravish on stage. Ravishing girl. Soon after the show closed (with rave reviews, I might add), I drove back to New York nonstop.

My return to New York was hardly triumphant. My 1971 Buick broke down on the New Jersey Turnpike on my way into the Holland Tunnel. I got it started again somehow and limped into town, white smoke spewing. And there I was, virtually broke, having been assured that my paycheck for the play's run would be along shortly by mail. I was homeless, too. Before I left for Florida, I had given up my studio apartment (as well as my New York girlfriend). I had also given up my job packing boxes in a kite factory. Yes, a kite factory. No job, no apartment, no money, no girlfriend. (But I was looking forward to seeing Michelle again before too long. Although she'd gone home to Coral Gables after our show, she planned to move to New York as soon as she could—and not because I was there, but because that's what she wanted.)

At least I was invited to crash at a friend's place. I went back to the kite factory to be told there were no jobs available. But the owners had taken a liking to me and told me to visit their friends who owned a cheese shop on the Upper East Side.

The rest is complete dumb luck. I worked there, at HQZ Cheese Pantry, for two years, fell into Dean & DeLuca and lasted two years, fell into Pasta & Cheese and lasted about six months.

That's when my friend Richie tipped me off about this market on the Upper West Side. He was in charge of the cheese department there and was making a heck of a lot more money than I was. He was leaving to pursue the notion of opening his own shop. So I had an interview with Howie Glickberg, one of the three owners.

There it was—Fairway Market. Midblock, sandwiched between a hippie clothing store and a coffee shop.

So in 1980, I became the thirty-year-old guy behind the cheese counter at Fairway. It is a city health requirement that people working at food counters have to wear some kind of hat. We had no Fairway caps in those days, and despite the fact that I was a pretty avid Yankees fan and had been all my young life, I chose to wear a St. Louis Cardinals baseball cap. In those days, nobody except ballplayers wore baseball caps. But I grew up in

Columbia, Missouri, 123 miles from St. Louis, a two-hour straight shot east on Interstate 70. My dad and my granddad took me to the Cardinals' games. So for no particular reason other than to make a feeble attempt to hang on to my roots, I'd wear my Cardinals cap. I'd show up at six or seven in the morning and commence setting up the department. This was a painstaking, arduous task that rarely took less than three hours. You see, every night when the store would close at eleven, all my little chèvres and other fragile cheeses had to be shrouded in flimsy bakery tissue, gently placed back in their wooden boxes, and stored beneath the refrigerated coffin cases or in a walk-in refrigerator in the basement. The next morning they would all have to be hauled back up or out from underneath and laid out in a particular place, order, and style. The chèvres were innumerable, and several of each species sat on French rye straw mats all day, being continually replaced as they were sold. No other shop merchandised cheese in this fashion, except for the counters where I had already established cheese departments.

Before Fairway, cheeses were displayed in plastic wrap, usually behind glass. *Ne me touchez pas.* But the thing is—I intuited this early on—plastic wrap is injurious to serious cheeses. Certainly it would injure small cheeses that were still maturing, from when they were boxed and sold at the Rungis market, south of Paris, to when they were packaged and loaded onto container ships at Le Havre for the ten-day journey to Port Elizabeth, New Jersey, to when they were unloaded and hauled to a warehouse before being trucked to Fairway. All these diminutive cheeses were living and breathing. They'd suffocate if they were wrapped in plastic. The wrap is necessary for larger cheeses that have been cut, though. These cheeses surely evolve, too, but at a much slower and less evident pace. Plastic wrap keeps their exposed faces from oxidizing.

My display method was one I learned from the master cheesemongers of France, where cheese is treated like any other edible—it's laid out right under the noses of prospective customers. No matter whether a food is fish

Roasted Peppers with Fresh Chèvre

6 servings

One of my favorite dishes, and the building block for a great sandwich.

1. Preheat the oven to 500°F.
2. Place the whole peppers on a rimmed baking sheet and roast, turning once or twice, until the pepper skins are blistered and charred all over, 20 to 30 minutes.
3. Transfer the peppers to a brown paper bag. Close the bag and let the peppers steam until cool enough to handle, at least 5 minutes. Peel the peppers and cut them in half lengthwise, removing and discarding the charred skin, stems, and seeds.
4. Lay the pepper halves on a serving platter, alternating colors. Drizzle the olive oil and red wine vinegar over them. Dot them with the chèvre and sprinkle with the garlic slices. Season with salt and pepper. Garnish with a few parsley leaves.

3 large red bell peppers

3 green (or yellow) bell peppers

3 to 4 tablespoons extra-virgin olive oil

1 to 2 teaspoons red wine vinegar, to taste

4 ounces fresh chèvre

1 garlic clove, peeled and very thinly sliced (use a mandoline or truffle shaver, if available)

Kosher or sea salt and freshly ground black pepper, to taste

Leaves from 1 sprig flat-leaf parsley, for garnish

Chef's Note: Don't overdo the garlic. This dish is not about the sharp taste of raw garlic. Instead, the garlic should be an accent to the sweetness of the peppers and the creamy tang of the goat cheese. For a terrific sandwich, layer the peppers and chèvre on sliced baguette or a ciabatta roll and season as described above with olive oil, vinegar, garlic slivers, sea salt, and pepper.

or chocolate, pastries or berries, the European sensibility was and is the correct one. No edible is so precious that it should be cloistered as if one needs an appointment to regard it. I suppose it was this immediacy, this palpable, irresistible availability, the myriad shapes and sizes and colors, that made me so devoted to my cheeses. You become very attached, curatorial, certainly protective of your medium in any field, and I was no stranger to this obsessive husbandry. I was like a brooding hen in my zeal to nurture and at the same time show off my progeny.

Fairway was only about 3,000 square feet when I started working there, and the decor was bare-bones. Okay, it had no decor; just bin after bin of fruits and vegetables, a few refrigerated cases for deli and cheese items, and floor dumps of boxes that were opened with razor cutters to display various things—crackers, cans, bottles—often the sort of hippie-dippie health food that Howie Glickberg brought into the shop in a shrewd and ultimately successful attempt to appeal to the Upper West Side mentality of the day. The cheese department was all the way in the back, made up of a refrigerated shelved stand-up unit with an eight-foot refrigerated "coffin" case in front of it. Along the wall to the right were two more eight-foot refrigerated coffin cases in which precut, wrapped, weighed, and priced chunks of various cheeses and the occasional piece of halvah were merchandised in vertical lines according to color—orange, white, orange, white, halvah, white, chocolate halvah, orange, and so forth. It was a cheese display that can be described only as workmanlike, as opposed to the levels and landscapes of Brueghelian and Fra Lippo Lippian majesty I had assembled every morning at Dean & DeLuca and, to a lesser degree, at Pasta & Cheese.

Fairway's owners had nailed two-by-fours to the top backs of each of these coffin cases in order to display various nuts and dried fruits in big glass canisters. Behind these coffin cases was an aisle where, all day, six days a week, Kenny Jones and Jerry Bonaparte would cut, wrap, weigh, and

price chunks of cheese, which they then dropped into milk cases and, at intervals, hauled around to the front of the refrigerators in order to replenish the stock. "Packing out," we call it. (Kenny and Jerry still work at Fairway, I might add.)

The aisle where Kenny and Jerry did their work was a constant clutter, a waist-high riot of full and empty boxes of cheese, nuts, and dried fruit. In order to cross it to give a customer half a pound of cashews, one had to swim—nay, flail—down this rock-filled, chest-high, storm-swollen creek bed. I have never seen anything like it. I had essentially been ripped from the urbane, everything-has-its-place, serene, haughty world of fancy food and thrust headlong into a peasantlike, sawdust-on-the-floor, "we'll sell anything that sells" commoners' market. I had no idea how perfect my situation was turning out to be. Not to mention the fact that even in these early days (this was 1980; Harold and David joined Howie to become involved with the business in 1972), the store was always crowded—much more so than any other shop I'd ever worked in.

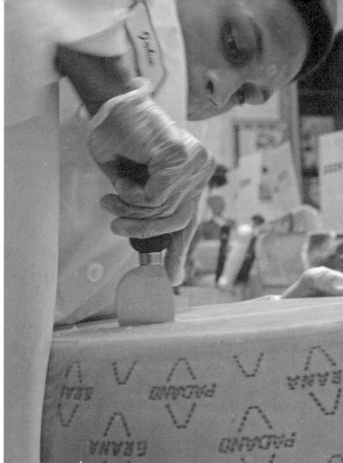
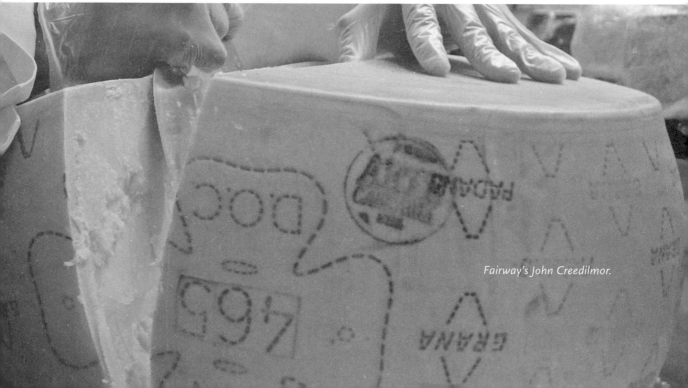

Fairway's John Creedilmor.

A *Maître Fromager* Is Born

The year I started at Fairway, I was contacted out of the blue by the Guilde des Fromagers, Confrérie de Saint-Uguzon—the French master cheesemongers' guild in Dijon. I was to be the first American inducted into the guild. At a ceremony in a hotel in Paris that autumn, I was installed as a *compagnon,* the neophyte level. Now, twenty-eight years later, I am a *prud'homme,* the highest status. Uguzon, I learned, is the patron saint of herdsmen. During the Middle Ages, certain professions organized guilds in order to further the study and knowledge of their craft. A few of these ancient guilds, like the Confrérie de Saint-Uguzon, have survived. Seven hundred years ago, this guild was for cheesemakers, and in 1969 it was revived as a fraternity for those in the business of curating fine cheese. (Despite the name "fraternity," it is no longer male-dominated—there are several respected female master cheesemongers.)

These European guilds place a lot of emphasis on pomp, formality, tradition, and ceremony. We wear long velvet robes, feathered medieval hats, and wide-ribboned sashes attached to gaudy ceremonial medallions. Silly, but lovable. And effective. All this keeps the profession together and makes a lot of deserving overachievers feel good about themselves.

In 1982 I was the first American to be inducted into another French master cheesemongers' brotherhood, the honorary Taste-Fromage. Taste-Fromage is more a distinction than a working guild. But it looks good on a résumé.

The daily setup routine may have been time-consuming, but it served a number of purposes. First, by the time I, along with two or three people on my morning counter staff, finished, this area of the store was among the most dramatic, exciting, and—in terms of sales—effective visual displays anyone could have the privilege of visiting without paying an admission fee.

The routine also served to season and educate my counter help. All morning, every morning, I would talk about food and cheese with them and with any customer who asked a question or merely wanted to talk about our stuff. This constant banter and repartee created within our business a climate where food and cheese were primary. You don't get that in most food shops and stores in this country—at least you didn't in those days. The routine also provided a practical education in cheese: the nature, care, and handling of all cheeses, not just the little chèvres. Seventy-pound forms of Parmigiano had to be rolled out of the walk-in refrigerators, several every day, in order to be brought to room temperature (a cold Parmigiano is so hard it would take explosives to get through the rind) so that they could be split, split again, split yet again, and finally split into sixteenths, from which consumer-size

continued on next page

chunks could be sold. I had to teach everyone how to do it. The task requires specially made knives that can be wedged into the Parmigiano, jimmied and wiggled into it, then rocked back and forth and twisted until the cheese splits. And 220-pound wheels of Emmentaler from France and Switzerland had to be halved and quartered and cut into eighths—these massive convex shapes had to be cut with piano wire, which I bought, snipped into lengths, and attached to four-inch pieces of dowel rod. Some cheese had to be grated and put into containers. Mozzarella had to be taken out of its brine or water, wrapped in plastic, weighed, and priced. Cheeses in the shelved wall refrigerators had to be "faced" (scraped with a cheese plane), rewrapped, and replaced on the shelves. Five-pound wheels of Brie, upwards of two dozen a day, had to be cut into wedges, wrapped, weighed, priced, crammed back into their circular wooden boxes, then stacked up as high as was practicable on barrels that stood in front of the coffin cases. The tasks of running a cheese counter are endless and, though repetitive, serve to create a collegial bond among those who work there—not to mention making the department a trim little ship with everything screwed down tight and nothing flapping around. My bosses had really never seen anything like it. To them, the only segment of their business that required such labor-intensiveness was fruits and vegetables. But in truth, fruits and vegetables are no more complex than the Dewey decimal system in a library. Apples and pears are sturdy and finite and not terribly troublesome—like a clutter of mislaid books as compared with the fragility and curatorial mothering required of any self-respecting cheese department.

So I soon got over feeling as though Fairway was beneath me. The truth was that Fairway was so far over my head it was ridiculous. This was how food should be sold at retail. No matter how rare, expensive, or fragile a foodstuff was, this was how to handle it. *Abbondanza*. A great quantity unceremoniously piled up and shamelessly proclaiming its wonderment by a handmade sign stapled to a cucumber crate slat sharpened to a point and thrust violently into its midst. A sign that shouted its name with copy that validated its existence—what it was, where it came from, why it was famous, how it is best used, how we (I) came across it, how its closest imitator is an out-and-out phony unworthy of your attention, why you must immediately buy an armload of it. A sign unafraid to get in your face, challenge you to deny that you frequently make bad choices, and affirm that this would not be one of them—"FRESH BLACK FIGS, RAW SEX—SAME THING, 79 CENTS EACH"—a sign that shouts out the price in big red numerals so you'll believe how proud we are of selling at such a low price.

This was opposed to the boutique approach to food that was then the norm, not just in New York but all across the country. Food so rarefied it had to be behind glass. Food you mustn't touch. Food so noncommittal that it had no signage to explain its worth, because no one in that particular shop had any connection to it, no passion for it, no responsibility for its being there in the first place. And not just fresh food, but shelf items, too.

So I learned that every single thing in a Fairway has a story—has a certain remarkable, articulable significance, a potentially irresistible argument for finding its way into your pantry. So all these foodstuffs require, deserve, demand a sign. One result, obviously, is sales: increased and ever-increasing sales. Another result is an education for the shopper. I learned that if you can establish yourself as the authority for any or all the products you sell, you become a destination shop.

Following the lead of my bosses David, Howie, and Harold, and thanks to their support, over the next eight years I took my cheese operation at Fairway to local prominence and to stardom in the food world. That included not just the greatest and grandest assemblage of cheeses anywhere on the planet, certainly in New York, but also fresh pasta; fresh wild mushrooms; block butters from Normandy, Brittany, Poitou-Charentes, and upstate New York; bulk crème fraîche from Normandy; mascarpone from Lombardy; *mozzarella di bufala* from Campania; Ben's fresh, gumless cream cheese and baked farmer cheese and pot cheese. Stuff I had to have for myself. I sold olives from huge crocks that I dressed in the style of their origin. Food producers and cheesemakers began to show up, laden with their pride and joy, begging me to taste and pass judgment and give advice about how to improve their foodstuffs, dreaming that I would find their whatever-it-was good enough to sell at Fairway.

You must understand what a heady time it was for us and for people

FAIRWAY
"Like No Other Market"

FAIRWAY ITALIAN RED WINE VINEGAR

WE FOUND THIS WONDERFUL VINEGAR IN PIEDMONT. SO GOOD, IT SHOULD HAVE STAYED WINE! PLUS, IT'S CHEAP AS DIRT.

$1⁷⁹ 1 LITER

who were serious about food. These imported cheeses and dairy foods, these staples, had never before seen New York, and New Yorkers had never seen any of them without traveling outside the country. We changed everything. I stocked country hams from Missouri and Kentucky, live wild snails from Sicily that crawled all over the place, and *sopressata* (Calabrian-style salami) from Savoy Provisions down on Houston Street, as well as the glorious *salsiccia secca* (dry sausage), the almost Italian-tasting, chubby cured pork salami, spiked with black pepper or hot chiles, that has to be hung for a couple of months before it is "ripe," all the while dripping precious fat that must be taken into account before you apply a retail price to it. I got in *Bundnerfleisch,* the lean, luscious, air-dried beef from Switzerland. I ferreted out bakers in Brooklyn, Queens, and New Jersey in order to draw in customers daily. Once you're hooked on a certain baker's bread, there's no being without it.

Ben's Cheese Shop

Since 1977 I've been buying cream cheese, blocks of sweet butter, farmer cheese, and baked farmer cheese from Jonah Friedman, the owner of Ben's Cheese Shop. Ben's is a tiny retail dairy shop on Houston Street; it's been there forever. Jonah buys his stuff from a private dairy upstate, and he has steadfastly refused to tell what and where this dairy is. Commercial cream cheeses (and lots of other stuff) contain guar gum (a plant) or agar agar (a seaweed) or gum arabic (sap from a tree) as thickeners. But Ben's cream cheese is so rich in cream that it doesn't need any of these—it's gumless. The result is a more attractive mouthfeel.

When you run a destination shop, customers come from all over the area, not just the neighborhood. You've got to have a passion for and deep knowledge about your stuff. In my case, most of the stuff I was crazy about I had pioneered—I'd gone to a lot of trouble to get it into the store before anyone else ever thought about it. And once you enter this realm of gastronomy, one foodstuff begets another or relies on another in order for it to fulfill its mission, which is delight.

And brutally hard work. By 1988, I thought I was burned out in retail. Not only that, I had a cheese book to write. I was never going to get it done on my schedule. I was working long hours, to put it mildly. How could I possibly write a book too? So after eight years, I left Fairway. Michelle's and my children were very young, and my professional life couldn't have been better. You'd have to be out of your mind to turn your back on the situation I was in. Seemed logical to me at the time: go against all logical wisdom. What an idiot!

For the next eight years, I was a consultant. I was hired for innumerable fulfilling projects, learned a lot, made new friends, still earned enough to

Haricots Verts with Toasted Hazelnuts

Serves 4

Haricots verts fins, or "skinny green beans," became chic in New York in the late 1980s. They were indeed imported from France at first, but soon they were being grown in Guatemala, of all places, to supply restaurants and markets in the United States. Central American haricots are not a whit different from the French ones, and they are undeniably lovely. I vastly prefer them over ordinary string beans, or green beans, whichever name you're used to.

1 cup raw hazelnuts

1 tablespoon kosher or sea salt, plus additional to taste

1 pound haricots verts, trimmed

3 tablespoons unsalted butter, chilled

1. Bring a medium pot of water to a boil. Meanwhile, crush the hazelnuts on a cutting board with the back of a heavy pan or in a bag with a wooden mallet—the pieces should be no larger than peas.

2. In a dry, heavy pan over low heat, lightly toast the hazelnuts, stirring constantly, until they give off a nutty aroma, 3 to 5 minutes. Take the pan off the heat, leaving the nuts in the pan so they stay warm.

3. Once the water is boiling, add 1 tablespoon of salt and toss in the green beans. Cook the beans for 6 to 8 minutes, testing for doneness. (I hate al dente vegetables, but that's a life choice.) Drain well.

4. Add the drained beans to the pan with the toasted hazelnuts. Add the butter, return the pan to low heat, and stir until the butter has melted, coating the beans and nuts. Season with salt to taste.

Chef's Note: In my opinion, haricots verts are truly delicious only when *fully* cooked—none of that al dente nonsense here. And they're supposed to be a darker shade of green when they're cooked. If they're still bright green, they're raw. Also, keep in mind that nuts retain heat and will continue to darken for a few minutes after you remove the pan from the burner, so take them off before they look toasted.

support the family . . . but I felt like a prostitute. Still, I finished the cheese book. As it was about to be published, and all the book hoopla was about to begin, out of the blue, the phone rang. Michelle picked it up, and there was my ex-boss David Sneddon, to whom I have always been devoted. He says to her, "I'm going to save Steve's life."

They wanted me back.

Except for the births of our kids, I think this was the happiest day of my life.

2

The Ones Who Make It Happen:

Founders to Managers to Cashiers

Fairway didn't just appear out of the blue on the Upper West Side. Fairway has long been Fairway. Nathan Glickberg emigrated from Russia to Pittsburgh, Pennsylvania, in the 1920s before moving to New York in the early 1930s. After a short while Nathan and his wife, Mary, opened a fruit and vegetable store in the present location at 74th Street and Broadway in Manhattan. Nathan's son, Leo Glickberg, whom I worked with in the 1980s and knew well, worked in his dad's store until he joined the United States Army Air Corps at the time of World War II. Following his discharge, Leo opened up his own fruit and vegetable store at 82nd and Broadway. In 1954, Nathan and Leo consolidated their operations at the 74th Street store, adding groceries, meat, cheese, dairy products, and frozen foods to their already famous and doubtless

The Owners

Several years ago, John Rossi, who was then Fairway's general manager, found a black-and-white photo of three old men of Palermo, taken during the 1950s or 1960s. One of them was missing a leg, another an eye. All were missing teeth. But each had features that could be construed as resembling those of one of the three owners of Fairway, our bosses. So I had my graphics guys blow the photo up to about four feet by eight feet. I had it hung in the two (at that time) stores. I labeled each of the men with the corresponding name and added the title "Our Founders." Almost everyone, including Harold, Howie, and David, thought it was pretty funny. But then one West Sider complained that it was demeaning to the memory of the three old men. No matter that no one knew who they were, or ever would know. We took it down. Political correctness was invented on the Upper West Side, you know.

gorgeous produce displays. The store was called "Fairway," the name of a family-run business that manufactured stuffed animals and toys.

In 1974 Leo's son, Howard Glickberg, joined the family business and transformed the store from a typical supermarket operation into the formal beginnings of the high-end, low-price specialty store it is today. Over the years Howie and his partners David Sneddon and Harold Seybert nurtured the store into a sophisticated, trend-setting retail operation. Daniel Glickberg, Howie's son, joined the family business after graduating from college in 2005, and is taking over some of the day-to-day responsibilities. Each generation of Glickbergs has become more successful than the last.

The Fairway Market flagship store on 74th Street was expanded from 3,500 square feet (when I first came to work here) to its present size, about 22,000 square feet. Additional New York Fairway stores have been built in West Harlem, Manhattan, in 1995; Plainview, Long Island, in 2001; and Red Hook, Brooklyn, in 2006. Fairway Market was named one of the country's six Outstanding Specialty Food Retailers in 2007.

Howie, David, and Harold are held almost in reverence by people in our business, and not just for their success, but for their performances as good people. I have never known three guys who got along as well as they have for all these years.

Howard Glickberg is about five years older than I am. He's the one who hired me—and he did it after a very short interview. "I can tell you're a good guy," he said. Howie grew up in the Bronx and then went to C. W. Post, majoring in finance. Out of college, he worked on Wall Street, where he was bored out of his mind. He made a change in his career and chose to take over the moldering old Upper West Side grocery store, Fairway, that his grandfather Nathan Glickberg had opened in the 1930s. Nathan had named it Fairway because that was the name of the family-run stuffed animal and toy manufacturing business.

Howie proved to be an astute businessman and an excellent merchandiser, despite having to labor under the unrelenting and

Mary Glickberg, Nathan's wife, in front of the original Broadway store.

critical eye of his father, Leo, whom I knew well. As a result, he has been increasingly successful for a long time and is the driving force behind Fairway. He is a good and devoted husband and father and also a devout and accomplished fisherman. He keeps his sizable fishing boat, *Jinx,* in Montauk, where he and his wife, Nita, have a lovely house.

Captain Howie is known out in Montauk as *the* tuna fisherman. Year after year, he seems to haul in the biggest tuna of the season—we're talking about 1,000-pound bluefins and huge bigeyes—not to mention a constant issue of yellowfins and albacores. Sharks, too, makos and blues. Japanese businessmen meet him right at the dock after he returns from his round-

trip, typically fifty to seventy-five miles out, where the big fish are. The tuna is flown to Tokyo that very day. Howie is a conservationist these days, and has been, actually, for several years. Dwindling tuna stock has him fishing for more plentiful species.

Harold Seybert is the oldest of the big three. Harold is from Philadelphia, but he moved to New York when he was young and has remained in the area ever since. Like Howie, he is an avid fisherman. Harold has always been in the produce business. His father, like Howie's, operated a market. In the 1960s, Harold became a tomato jobber. He purchased truckloads of premium tomatoes from various sources and sold them to grocery stores up one avenue and down another. This went on for years. A lucrative business, doubtless. He and his partner and brother-in-law, David Sneddon, drove the truck as well as schlepped the heavy cases of tomatoes into the various stores. Harold and David became friendly with Howie and his father, and one day Howie proposed that they come into Fairway as equal partners. The two men jumped at the opportunity, and the rest is history. Each complements the others beautifully.

Harold established himself early on as a consummate merchandiser, retailer, and buyer of fruits and vegetables. He has won every award the produce industry offers. It didn't hurt that even before 1980, when I joined the company, Harold had already hired my current partner and colleague, Peter Romano, as his right-hand man. Peter made his way to Manhattan, and Fairway, from Italy; he was born on the island of Lampedusa, between Sicily and Tunisia. These days, he is 100 percent responsible for our produce business—and let me tell you, he works like a draft horse even now. Peter

Me, Paul Weiner (organic boss), Angelo (Anchovy) Costagliola (butcher, Ray's #1).

Thomas Hurt, Carl Small, and Trent Johnson—Fairway delicatessen and appetizing guys
(each is an expert smoked salmon–slicer).

Longtime Fairway produce guy Jaime Figueroa.

Brenda, me, Adrese, Henry, and Jacka at our Red Hook (Brooklyn) store; Brenda works in the deli with Henry, who is the best smoked salmon–slicer I have ever known; Adrese Harris is our excellent cheese department manager; and Jacka makes fresh mozzarella for us at a glass-fronted counter right in the midst of Fairway shoppers.

performs extraordinary feats of strength (potatoes and onions are heavy!) hour after hour, six or seven days a week, year after year.

Harold, along with David and Howie, who also must be considered consummate produce men, taught Peter everything he knows about fruits and vegetables—most importantly, how produce should be displayed. Every pear with a wadded-up piece of tissue (tissue is packed with pears in their boxes) nestled between it and the next one. Towering displays of apples and melons. Magnificent seasonal shows of, alternately, pumpkins, strawberries, melons, radishes—produce merchandised in a manner that promotes ever-increasing sales.

A born and bred New Yorker, David Sneddon lived mostly in Brooklyn during his youth but has lived in Manhattan all his adult life. His sensibility, his taste for European food, and his New York style have helped to make Fairway the serious food store that it is. And this is crucial to understanding Fairway, because David, like Harold and Howie, is old-school.

What do I mean by old-school? You coddle no one who works for you. You stack it high and sell it cheap. You know that no sign (on, in, or near a product display) means no sale. Get a sign on that stuff, for heaven's sake. Never give people a raise to inspire them; give a raise only when it's been earned. There's no such thing as a half-day. A workday is all day. And eight hours is not a workday—it's merely two-thirds of a workday. Holidays are workdays. Take time off when it's not so busy. Plow as much money as necessary back into the business for improvements or whatever; you'll get it back in spades. Trust no one. Everyone is capable of stealing (and people often do steal). Never make the same mistake twice. One way to avoid this?—Never give second chances. That means never forgive a shoplifter—once shoplifters are caught, never allow them back in, no matter how contrite they are. Never rehire somebody you've fired. Vendors too: if one cheats you, he's out. Forever. That'll teach 'im.

And—maybe most important—never be afraid to try something new. Trust your instincts. Dare to make a statement with something not ordinar-

Sautéed Striped Bass on Israeli Salad

The foundations of Fairway were laid in the produce department—after all, for a lot of people the store is Salad Central. I've done my part, bringing in the oils and vinegars for dressings, in large part to complement the superb produce department created by our founders. This salad is at its best in the summer, when tomatoes are at their peak.

1 cup peeled, diced seedless cucumber

1 cup diced, seeded ripe tomato

½ cup diced red onion

¼ cup chopped scallions

¼ cup chopped flat-leaf parsley

5 tablespoons fresh lemon juice

¼ cup plus 2 tablespoons extra-virgin olive oil

Kosher or sea salt and freshly ground black pepper

4 to 8 deboned striped bass fillets (about 2 pounds fish)

1. In a large bowl, mix the cucumber, tomato, and red onion with the scallion, parsley, 4 tablespoons of the lemon juice, and ¼ cup of the olive oil. Season with salt to taste. Set the salad aside.

2. Heat 1 tablespoon of the remaining olive oil in a large pan over medium-high heat until hot but not smoking. Sprinkle the fillets with salt and pepper and place in the pan skin-side up. Sauté the fish over medium heat until just opaque, about 2 minutes on each side for ½-inch-thick fillets. Transfer to a plate to stop the cooking.

3. Mound the salad in the center of each plate and top with fish. Drizzle the fillets with the remaining tablespoon of olive oil and the remaining tablespoon of lemon juice and serve immediately.

Fishmonger's Note: Of course you needn't limit this recipe to striped bass. But, really, there is no better-tasting fish.

Rustic Apple Tart with Crème Fraîche

Serves 6

Mitchel's rustic apple tarts are as close to perfection as anything I have ever experienced (so are his cupcakes, but you'll have to go to his restaurant to try those). He has the touch of a gastronomic autodidact, a knack that can't be taught, of infusing even classics like this tart with a delicious intensity that makes them his own.

1. Preheat the oven to 400°F. Spread the apple wedges on two rimmed baking sheets and toss each with half the granulated sugar (this is best done with bare hands, to avoid making a mess). Dot each pan with 1½ tablespoons of the cold butter. Roast the apples, tossing to coat with the butter and reversing the pans back to front and top to bottom halfway through, until the apples are tender and slightly colored in spots, 25 to 35 minutes. (When done, the apple wedges should be soft, but not applesauce—they should still retain their shape.) Transfer the pans to a rack and let cool thoroughly, about 45 minutes.

2. Roll out the defrosted puff pastry to a circular shape approximately 14 inches in diameter and ¼ inch thick. Don't be concerned if your circle isn't perfect; that's where the rusticity comes in!

3. Line a clean, cool baking sheet with parchment paper or a nonstick liner. Transfer the puff pastry disk to the lined pan.

4. In a large bowl, toss the roasted apples with the brown sugar. Spread them over the puff pastry, leaving a 1½-inch border of pastry uncovered. Dot the apples with the remaining 2 tablespoons of butter. Fold the puff pastry border back over the apples, overlapping as you go. This will leave a large area of apples showing in the center of the tart. Use a pastry brush to paint the surface of the puff pastry with the beaten egg.

5. Bake the tart until the pastry is deeply golden, about 45 minutes. Transfer to a wire rack and let cool slightly, for about 10 minutes. Slice and serve warm with a dollop of crème fraîche on each plate.

10 Golden Delicious apples, cored, peeled, and cut into eighths

¼ cup granulated sugar

5 tablespoons unsalted butter, chilled and diced

¾ pound prepared puff pastry, defrosted according to package instructions (see Chef's Note)

¼ cup light brown sugar

1 large egg, lightly beaten

Crème fraîche, for serving

Chef's Note: Transferring a puff pastry tart to a wire rack will allow it to cool better than leaving it on the baking sheet. By letting the air circulate beneath the dough, the rack keeps it crisp. By the way, puff pastry tarts reheat beautifully: return the tart to the sheet pan and bake for 5 minutes at 350°F.

Grocer's Note: Prepared puff pastry is available in the frozen section of any well-stocked market and is a perfectly acceptable alternative to making the pastry from scratch. Choose the all-butter kind for the richest flavor.

ily found in a supermarket—tiny $150 bottles of balsamic vinegar? Why not see how they go? Olive oil pressed from olives grown in your own groves in Umbria? Worth a shot. Want to learn about catering and kitchens? Start a separate catering business.

So David is definitely old-school, but with a "new-school" mentality. He knew what to do to make Fairway a memorable shopping experience. He knew there had to be more to it than fruits and vegetables. It was David who goaded me to follow my instinct, because he might just support some of my crazy ideas. David also taught me that there was no reason to rely on local importers and distributors. We could do it all ourselves. After all, food and Europe are our hobbies. Our lust for serious food should be enough to inspire us to source and import everything we want. Let's boil and bake our own bagels. Let's smoke our own salmon. Let's roast our own coffee. Let's cook our own food. If you want it done right, you have to do it yourself.

STEVE'S BLOG OF THE DAY
February 7, 2007

It seems that some of you are actually taking *Top Chef*, the Bravo network TV show, seriously. Astonishing. I've not been a witness to such drivel and nonsense since I can't remember when. I mean, I can enjoy the lowbrow as much as the next person. But this stuff makes my skin crawl. And I sat there like a lump and took it in, as a professional responsibility, of course. Several times I became aware that my mouth was hanging open, and not because of any gustatory desire but rather because I was a witness to this stupidity. So it came down to the announcement of the *Top Chef* on Wednesday night—would it be Ilan or Marcel?—and I got up and walked away from it, without a second thought as to who the winner would be. Had I stayed for the announcement it would be fair to call me a hypocrite. I'm already a hypocrite, so that's no threat.

Before I say anything more, I want to tell you about Mitchel—Mitchel London. He's a New York chef, and he operates the café and steakhouse at our flagship store at Broadway and 74th Street. All the recipes in this book are his. The café and steakhouse were David's idea.

He and his wife, Carmela, have run their own takeout shops and catering business, Mitchel London Foods, for twenty years or so, and during that time Mitchel has built up a mystique about himself that is unique, at least among high-profile chefs. He dislikes just about everything having to do with the food scene. He loathes the notion of "celebrity" chefs and harbors a distaste for New York restaurants, with the

Zabar's

Zabar's has been a neighbor of Fairway all these years; it's only six blocks up Broadway from the flagship store and is a New York institution. Zabar's specializes in "appetizing," which is New Yorkese for food Jewish people like to eat, stuff they were all raised on, but totally foreign to a midwestern gentile like me—smoked salmon; pickled herring; smoked sturgeon; and sable, which is actually black cod, I eventually learned. It's funny that the two stores have coexisted so unrancorously all these years. It is well-known, and in part documented, that I detest any store that considers itself a competitor of Fairway. But our relationship with Zabar's and its partners has always been more than civil. We have always had and always will have a great deal of respect for them. In the old days, they specialized in smoked fish and fresh-roasted coffee and kitchenware (batterie de cuisine) and housewares, and we specialized in fruits and vegetables. They've got a great store . . . but it ain't a Fairway.

exception of his hardly private haunts, Jean-Georges and the Four Seasons. J-G I can understand, because the food and service are superb. But the Four Seasons, the landmark Midtown restaurant designed by Philips Johnson, is about as unfashionable, if not stodgy, as you can get. Still, Mitchel insists that he frequents it not so much because the food delights him but because of the ambience and the fact that Julian Niccolini, one of the owners, knows and accommodates him.

Mitchel London knows from fresh eggs. He knows from butter and crème fraîche. He falls to his knees before ice cream, hot dogs, and corned beef hash. Milk shakes are a particular passion, and as he often says, "They go down way too easy." Mitchel hates fussiness, heaps scorn on "fusion," has no respect for anything gimmicky, and becomes oddly childlike at the prospect of sitting before a *croque-monsieur* of his own making. His passion is the old way, the old dishes made with ingredients that are unassailable. He knows jack about cheese, but he knows what he likes, primarily French cheeses—real Camembert and real Brie (artisanal examples, as opposed to factory-made), and serious chèvres, though I am delighted that he admits the primacy of Parmigiano-Reggiano. Throughout the journey on which Mitchel's

A Future Chef's Midnight Snacking Habits

When he was fifteen, Mitchel went to a boarding school near Netanya, while his mom stayed in Tel Aviv. She told him one day that he should devote his life to food. This *nudzh* was largely lost on a teenager. Not too long after Elaine delivered this advice, though, he found himself sneaking out of his dorm in the wee hours with a bunk mate, hiking to a nearby field of romaine lettuce, climbing the tall fence, ripping heads of romaine out of the ground, and spiriting them back to the dorm kitchen. Then he slunk out to the school's chicken coop, climbed *that* fence, swiped as many eggs as he could carry, and spirited *them* back to the kitchen. . . . Thereupon, using the kitchen's olive oil, he proceeded to whip up fresh mayonnaise and combine it with ketchup to make Russian dressing to toss with the fresh, warm romaine.

He says he pulled this caper numerous times. And he further confesses to being unable to explain how he knew how to make fresh mayonnaise—instinctively, he supposes. I asked him if this was a sort of epiphany, a turning point in his life, a light going on. He says no, he was more amazed not to have been shot, because in that part of the world at that time with that many armed Israeli soldiers on guard, sneaking around in the middle of the night was probably not a good idea.

food life has taken him (the only life he has, I might add), France stands as the definition of how to get food-related things done the right way. It must be said that Mitchel's respect for and execution of a number of Italianate pasta dishes is just one of the anomalies that add up to this Francophile's standing as the best cook I've ever known. Normandy butter is another passion of his, and though it is not a cheese, Mitchel considers it one. I once heard it said that Italians believe the best French cheese is Normandy butter.

Mitchel was the chef for Edward I. Koch, one of the best mayors New York ever had. (Koch shops at Fairway all the time, by the way.) Mitchel cooked for him at the mayor's residence, Gracie Mansion, a lovely old house that sits on a dramatic rise overlooking Hell Gate, the turbulent convergence of the East River with the Harlem River and Long Island Sound. Mitchel got a lot of press then, and that is when I first took notice of him. After all, major newspaper reports about goings-on in city government don't ordinarily mention what the mayor's chef served at this or that meeting or supper.

No matter. Mitchel was the reason venerable food shops such as Dean & DeLuca and Balducci's got kudos for their pastry departments. His pastries—rustic apple tarts, cheesecakes, a few other diminutive confections—were the backbone of the operations at these two famous stores. His cheesecakes were a passion of and cash cow for Zabar's great impresario, the recently deceased Murray Klein, with whom, if it could be said that Mr. Klein was close to anybody, Mitchel was close.

Mitchel lived in Israel during his teens. There they were, settled in Philly, and one day his mother, Elaine, said, "We're moving to Israel." Her decision had nothing to do with religion or spirituality. According to Mitchel, it was more about spontaneity than anything else. And life in Israel and the Middle East was at least as tumultuous then as it is now. The experience served to foment and crystallize for Mitchel a great deal of his attitude toward and passion for serious food, whether he knew it or not at the time. One of the few things Mitchel likes about me is the fact that I am so zealously pro-Israel, as is he. Politics aside, he makes the best hummus I've ever tasted, a legacy of his time in Israel.

So when I regard a product for possible inclusion in the vaunted Fairway product mix, I always filter it through Mitchel London's sensitivity apparatus. What would Mitchel say? Gimmicky? Contrived? Or more serious, worthy? Mitchel's never wrong. Except for that night in the Fairway steakhouse a few years ago when a one-legged patron put his cigarette out on Mitchel's forehead. (This sounds incredible, but I assure you it happened. The guy lit up, then went ballistic when Mitchel told him to snuff it.)

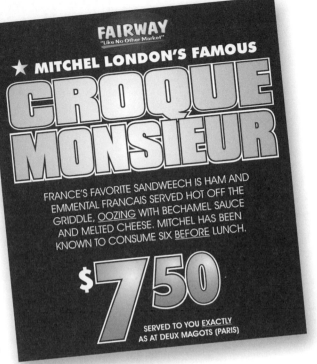

FAIRWAY
"Like No Other Market"

★ MITCHEL LONDON'S FAMOUS

CROQUE MONSIEUR

FRANCE'S FAVORITE SANDWEECH IS HAM AND EMMENTAL FRANCAIS SERVED HOT OFF THE GRIDDLE, OOZING WITH BECHAMEL SAUCE AND MELTED CHEESE. MITCHEL HAS BEEN KNOWN TO CONSUME SIX BEFORE LUNCH.

$750

SERVED TO YOU EXACTLY AS AT DEUX MAGOTS (PARIS)

Every spring, in late May or early June, Mitchel decamps to the south of France for three weeks. Carmela travels with him, and they take a villa with a pool, usually someplace close to the sea outside Saint-Tropez. Mostly what they do is shop, cook, and eat, apparently. He seems to call me every day to say something to this effect: "Steven. I have a problem. I'm sitting in front of a bowl of *fraises de bois* [wild strawberries, beyond sublime], and this crème fraîche is so thick I can't get it off the spoon." Or, "Steven. I just had a *saucisson sec* [cured salami] that was made from *marcassin* [young wild boar]." Or, "Steven. I can't decide which is better—this *brandade de morue* [salt cod whipped up with Provençal olive oil and garlic] I'm eating or the toasted bread I'm dipping in it."

But Mitchel's domain is the café and the steakhouse. What about the people who run the store itself? Each of the departments at Fairway is operated by a tried-and-true manager. All the managers started out as clerks, counter persons, stockers, cashiers. Most were at Fairway for years before they were blessed with the opportunity to manage. When they finally jumped at the promotion, they had the confidence that comes with having been steeped in the innumerable details of their particular operation. If it was food-related, as opposed to working in the front end, they were pretty well-versed in the nature of their food.

Let me give you an example—I'm probably the best example, but let's skip over me for the time being and take a look at, say, our prepared-food whiz, John.

John Rossi is about my age, or a little younger. He was born and raised in Philly. He came to Fairway soon after I left for an eight-year sabbatical between 1988 and 1996, to write my cheese book. John lived in Calabria for a number of years before he came to New York in the early 1980s. He was, is, undeniably, "downtown," an artsy, musical, foodie type of person. He was also a hipster (like me), street-smart and not afraid of anything (*not* like me). He opened and ran his own peasantlike restaurant for a few years, but

Classic Creamy Mashed Potatoes

Serves 6 to 8

Mitchel takes mashed potatoes very seriously, so when this recipe showed up, I was elated. I mean, you can screw up mashed potatoes. Wrong potato, not enough milk or butter—and you can end up with something lumpy, cold, gluey. Mitchel nails this dish, which is all too often tossed off. Take notes.

1. Heat enough water in a large pot to completely cover the cubed potatoes. Add a pinch of salt. Boil until the potatoes are thoroughly cooked and fork-tender, about 13 minutes. Drain the potatoes and transfer them to the bowl of an electric mixer fitted with the whisk attachment. Beat on medium-low speed, scraping down the sides of the bowl, until the potatoes are totally smooth and *no lumps remain*.

2. Add the heavy cream, ½ cup at a time, pouring slowly and mixing in each addition completely so that the potatoes have time to absorb the liquid. Scrape down the sides of the bowl between additions. Season the potatoes with the salt and freshly ground white pepper.

3. Return the potatoes to the pot and reheat over a low flame, stirring with a wooden spoon or a rubber spatula. Stir in the cold butter until melted and serve.

1½ teaspoons kosher or sea salt, plus a pinch for the cooking water

4 large Idaho potatoes (about 3 pounds), peeled and cut into large cubes

1 cup heavy cream

Freshly ground white pepper, to taste

4 tablespoons cold unsalted butter

Chef's Note: You can make these potatoes using a hand mixer or even a manual potato masher, but you'll never get them as creamy or smooth as with an electric KitchenAid-type mixer.

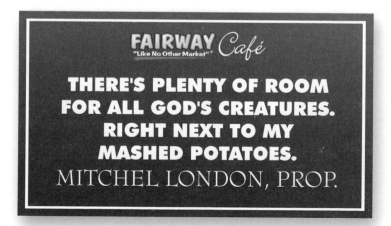

that's another story. John came to Fairway on a whim and interviewed with the owner David Sneddon. According to David, at this interview John was so truthful about himself and his past that David almost didn't hire him.

But John did get the job, and he set about doing whatever David told him to do. He stocked shelves with dry goods, worked the front end, and performed menial tasks that were way beneath him and totally removed from his job skills, which were all kitchen-oriented. He stuck with it—though how, I can't imagine—until he began to make his presence felt. He and David began to turn Fairway into a world-class market by adding kitchens and bakeries. David knew that unless we developed and excelled at prepared foods, breads and pastries baked on the premises, and coffees roasted in the store, Fairway would never move to the next level, the level where "just another food store" becomes a food hall extraordinaire. So it was John who faced the task of doing what David envisioned, and, by sheer luck, this was the same mental image John had. His European sensibility and downtown consciousness were the perfect match for David's desire to make Fairway special.

John is now master of a vast operation that includes cooks, chefs, bakers, kitchens, ovens, and all the perishable foodstuffs that make Fairway what it is—foodstuffs of a particular nature that can never be taken for granted or expected to be the same every day. Nothing makes itself, and the human element is perhaps most crucial when it comes to John's bailiwick. It requires constant scrutiny and a knack for divining the strengths and weaknesses of not just your key people, but your lowest-echelon workers.

When I assumed the role of "manager" of the Fairway cheese department in 1980, I was put in charge of a labor pool I had never imagined: untrained, unskilled people from all walks of life. I certainly never imagined working with people like this, much less communicating with them on a daily basis. But I got over that attitude in a hurry.

As it turned out, the thing I cherish most about Fairway is the thing that in the beginning freaked me out the most—the people I have had the privilege of working with, getting to know and trust them and in turn having them get to know and trust me. And you'd better believe I had to earn their trust. These were people from all over the city and all over the world, in contrast to the types of people I had worked with at the other shops—privileged, educated, mostly white kids, none of whom could hold a candle to anyone in my new crowd in terms of personality, life experience, ability, thirst for knowledge, professionalism, work ethic, or you name it. Maybe one in ten of the people I worked with at Fairway had a high school education.

When I came to Fairway, Broadway and the Upper West Side were entirely different from what they're like now. In those days, there were more homeless people around, and a lot of them shopped at Fairway. Some were bums by choice, and some were eccentrics and socialized schizophrenics, benign though clinically disturbed people. Most weren't really shoppers at all—maybe walk-arounders, just-looking-arounders: "So I've had three apples, two pears, and a half pint of rice pudding? So what? I was hungry. You'll never miss it."

Get out. Out. Do not come back.

But they came back. The next day. Hell, maybe later the same day as we loaded the shelves and glass-front refrigerator cases with the magic: the seventeen rare Tuscan and Umbrian olive oils, nine different Véritables Camemberts de Normandie, the first Prosciutto di San Daniele ever exported to the United States, freshly harvested lavender from a farm on Long Island.

This juxtaposition of the sublime and the ridiculous was Fairway. Still is.

Back in the 1980s we used to go through help pretty fast. That's not to say there aren't guys (and women) who have been working with us for twenty years, and we have plenty of them. But lots of jobs in the city are simply itinerant. Working as a porter or a deli clerk or a cashier is a transient situation.

We've seen them come; we've seen them go. People from all walks of life; of all ages, shapes, and sizes; and—most interesting, to me at least—from all countries. All the countries in Africa, Asia, Southeast Asia, South America, Central America, the Caribbean—you name it—have been represented at Fairway. Europe too, of course; we've had workers from Poland, Romania, Bulgaria, France, Scandinavia. Most countries of the world have been represented more than once. I can even remember most of the names of the people who've moved on.

Maybe my favorite names—and, coincidentally, two of my favorite guys—were Sooknarin and Roopnarin Sook-deo, brothers from Guyana and very talented deli workers. They could slice smoked salmon so thin you could read through it. I recently heard that Sooknarin had died, and the news made me very sad. Another kid was named Terence. From Suriname, right next to Guyana. Who'd have thought I would ever be close to someone from Suriname? Shy boy. Sweet. Spooky. He used to read at the counter instead of taking a lunch break. Would snap the book shut if he caught me trying to pick up the title.

And our cashiers: For a long time now, they've been an elegant cadre of impeccably clad West African women, the nicest, sweetest, funniest, most reliable, most accomplished, and efficient cashiers money can buy. A number of them make awfully good money because they are so proficient and have chosen to stay for so many years. Senegal, Sierra Leone, Gabon, Côte d'Ivoire. They know the Fairway regulars so well that each has a following. Fairway regulars' kids are a big part of this. For them, Fairway is an experience they will remember all their lives.

One of our top security guys, Jean (pronounced John) Kadende, tall and handsome—couldn't be more than twenty-eight—is so proficient and respected that he's making the transition from security to store management. He's from Burundi. (Am I boring you? This stuff is *important*.) Burundi! His family grows coffee, and I am determined to help him get it exported to us.

Curried Chickpeas

Serves 4

This dish is tasty and substantial enough to serve as a meal over steamed jasmine rice or basmati rice—or try it as an accompaniment to roasted meat. Plenty of fresh ginger and garlic give the sauce more depth than you'd expect from such a simple, meatless recipe.

1. Place the soaked, drained chickpeas in a large pot and cover with 3 quarts cold water; bring to a boil over medium-high heat. Boil for 10 minutes, skimming off any foam that collects on the surface. Add the onion, garlic, parsley, and olive oil.

2. Partially cover the pot and adjust the heat to keep the chickpeas at a slow, steady simmer until almost tender, about 45 minutes. Stir in the salt and continue simmering until the chickpeas are completely tender but not mushy, about 30 minutes more. Strain the chickpeas, reserving the cooking liquid; discard the onions, garlic, and parsley.

3. Bring a medium pot of water to a boil. Cut a small X in the bottom of each tomato. Drop the tomatoes into the boiling water for 20 seconds each to loosen the skins for peeling. Transfer the tomatoes to a bowl of cold water until they are cool enough to handle, then pull away the skins. Core, seed, and chop the tomato flesh.

4. Heat the vegetable oil in a large skillet over medium heat. Add the onion and cook, stirring, until well browned, 10 to 15 minutes. Lower the heat to medium-low and add the tomatoes with their juices, crushed garlic, ginger, coriander, cumin, salt, pepper, and bay leaf. Cook for 5 minutes, stirring a few times.

5. Add 1½ cups of the reserved chickpea broth to the skillet. Stir in the chickpeas, increase the heat to medium, and simmer until the liquid is reduced to a saucelike consistency, about 15 minutes. Serve sprinkled with chopped fresh cilantro.

CHICKPEAS:

1½ cups (12 ounces) dried chickpeas, soaked in cold water overnight, drained

1 medium onion, peeled and quartered

4 whole garlic cloves, peeled

2 sprigs flat-leaf parsley

1 tablespoon extra-virgin olive oil

2 teaspoons kosher or sea salt

SAUCE:

2 medium tomatoes

2 tablespoons vegetable oil

1 large onion, peeled and finely diced

3 garlic cloves, peeled and put through a press or finely grated

2 tablespoons grated fresh ginger

2 teaspoons ground coriander

2 teaspoons ground cumin

½ teaspoon kosher or sea salt

½ teaspoon freshly ground black pepper

1 bay leaf

1½ cups cooking broth from the chickpeas

Chopped fresh cilantro, for garnish

Grocer's Note: Since antiquity, spice merchants and home cooks have made their own proprietary spice blends, like the Middle Eastern *ras el hanout* or Indian garam masala. Experiment with your own, starting with the one-to-one blend of dried ground coriander and cumin in this recipe, then working in small quantities with other exotic seasonings like cayenne, ginger, cinnamon, and maybe a little ground dried rose petal. These chickpeas are a perfect canvas for good, fresh, fragrant spices of your choice.

The Meat Department,

Under the Command

of Master Butcher

Ray Venezia

airway has been blessed with uncanny good luck since the early 1970s. Things seem always to turn our way sooner or later. Most propitiously, we repeatedly come upon that one-in-a-million person who can overcome enormous challenges and help us to become the company we envision.

A perfect example is our master butcher, Ray Venezia. He is the reason we are considered the best in the business at meat and poultry, which we knew nothing about before we got into it in 1999. Actually, that process began a couple of years earlier. By 1998, Howie, Harold, and David were committed to making our business grow. In order to accomplish this, Howie insisted we had to do more than just open new Fairways—we had to be a one-stop market, where you could get everything. Another store in the neighborhood had recently made the transition from

being just a seafood shop to also offering meat and poultry, cheese, pastries, specialty groceries, and baked goods. Whole Foods was coming, too. It was clear that the competition was heating up. And the economy was booming. It was time to make our move. We found Ray through an industry consultant who knew him from his work at a family-owned market called Corrado's in New Jersey. Hiring him turned out to be one of the very best moves we ever made. He's solid gold.

Ray is a slender, handsome man pushing fifty, and probably three, maybe four generations from his family's roots in Sicily (not Venice, despite his last name). He was born and raised in New Jersey, and like his uncle, he became a butcher right out of high school, so that's a long career already. But in fact Ray is a dinosaur. There aren't many butchers like him anymore. The business of meat and poultry has been dramatically dumbed down from the days when the butcher was a crucial part of life. There was a time—as recently as thirty years ago—when your butcher knew just the right cut of meat for what you wanted to cook and knew how to persuade you to cook it. He would suggest meals that were spot-on bull's-eyes, and he made you feel special, looked-after. That butcher kept you coming back to his particular market (if he wasn't a freestanding butcher shop).

Just keeping a department like Ray's going is a monumental task. It is perhaps the toughest department to run in the entire retail food business, and certainly the toughest to run profitably. Classically, industry-wide, the average supermarket can expect no more than 10 percent of its gross dollars to come from meat and poultry, and of that fraction, an even smaller fraction is profit. The thing is this: meats and poultry are as perishable as seafood, and shoppers complain more about them and return more merchandise for refunds for whatever reason (some legit, some just cranky) than in any other department. Plus, throw in the complexities of offering kosher meat and poultry, and—well, just imagine.

These days, in nearly every supermarket in North America, the term "butcher department" is a misnomer. There are no butchers on the premises; there are just order-takers and wrappers. They can't be relied on for culinary advice. They know little or nothing of the anatomy of the animals, so don't expect them to be able to French a leg of lamb or bone-out a chicken for you. Suet for the bird feeder? What's suet? Ham hocks for the soup? What's a ham hock? Any veal bones for stock? What's stock? What's veal, for that matter? Their product comes to them already butchered to consumer size. Worse, much of it has been vacuum-packed. This is referred to as "boxed meat." No costly, time-consuming labor; no costly talent to be hired by the supermarket operator; no muss; no fuss.

Not so at Fairway—not with Ray in charge. Ray and his people perform every butchering task there is, short of actually dispatching live animals and birds. He says the most important thing a butcher department can do is offer peerless chopped meat. Recently, the reputation of chopped meat has been assailed repeatedly by recalls because of *E. coli* and salmonella

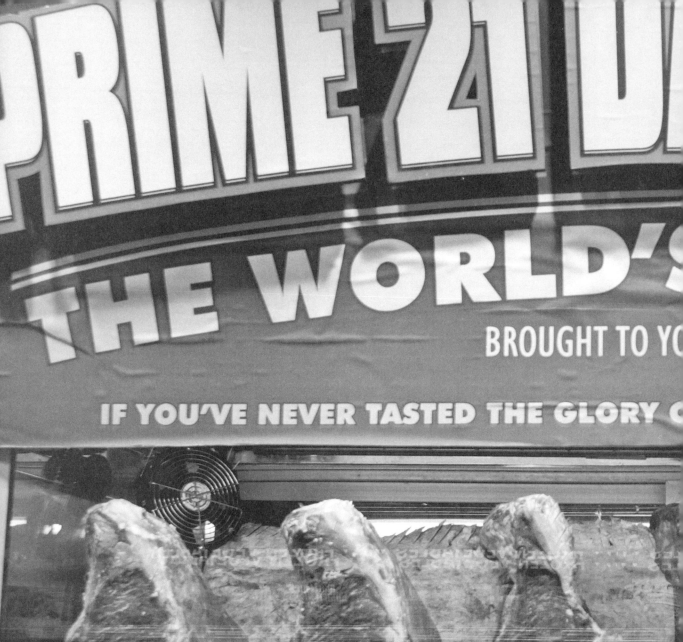

Pan-Roasted Tournedos
with Whole Garlic Cloves and Fresh Thyme

Serves 2

This dish is very quick and very easy and contains a lot of garlic—what could be better? Mitchel clarifies the butter because otherwise the milk solids will burn as you sear the meat.

2 slices fillet of beef tenderloin (each about 2 inches thick, about ¾ pound total; see Butcher's Note)

Kosher or sea salt and freshly ground black pepper to taste

4 tablespoons clarified butter (see Chef's Note)

1 whole head of garlic, cloves separated and smashed (skin left on)

8 sprigs fresh thyme

Coarsely chopped flat-leaf parsley, for garnish

1. Season the fillets with salt and pepper. Heat the butter in a cast-iron pan or another heavy-bottomed pan over medium heat. When the butter is hot, add the 2 fillets and cook them until dark golden brown, 3 to 5 minutes per side for medium-rare (the meat should feel just slightly resilient when pressed). Halfway through the cooking, add the garlic and thyme to the pan.

2. Transfer the fillets to warmed dinner plates. Top with the pan-roasted garlic and thyme. Pour butter from the pan over the fillets to taste. Sprinkle with parsley and season with additional salt, if desired.

Chef's Note: To clarify butter, melt it in a saucepan over very low heat. Continue to heat until the butterfat (clear golden liquid) has separated from the milk solids (opaque white liquid), which will sink to the bottom of the pan. Use a spoon to skim away all the froth that forms on the surface and discard the froth. With a small ladle or a large spoon, transfer the clear golden butterfat (clarified butter) to another container, taking care to leave the milk solids behind. Calculate that you will end up with about 7 tablespoons of clarified butter per stick of butter used.

Butcher's Note: Prime beef is worth every penny. Of all the beef consumed in North America, between 1 and 2 percent is graded prime (a small fraction of that is steakhouse-quality prime, twenty-one-day dry-aged beef). The difference between grades referred to as "select" (the lowest), "choice," and "prime" is immense.

Spicy Broiled Cornish Hens with Lemon and Fresh Oregano

Serves 2

These tangy, juicy Cornish hens are also delicious served hot over an arugula salad or steamed spinach. Use a gentle, fragrant olive oil here, like a taggiasca from Liguria, a Provençal oil, or an arbequina from Catalonia.

1. Butterfly the hens.
2. Chop about 1 tablespoon of fresh oregano leaves and reserve for garnish. In a large bowl, combine the remaining oregano sprigs with the olive oil, lemon juice, garlic, red pepper flakes, and ½ teaspoon salt. Put the hens in the bowl, turn them to coat with the marinade, and refrigerate for 4 to 6 hours.
3. Preheat the broiler. Remove and discard the oregano sprigs from the marinade and scrape most of the garlic from the hens. Transfer the birds, skin-side up, to a rimmed baking sheet or shallow roasting pan and drizzle each bird with 2 tablespoons of the marinade. Broil about 4 inches from the heat source until the skin is golden brown, about 7 minutes. Turn the hens and continue to broil until the chicken is golden on the second side, 8 to 10 minutes. Turn the chickens once more and continue to broil, basting every few minutes with the pan juices, until the skin is well browned and the juices run clear when the thigh is pierced, about 5 minutes more.
4. Transfer the hens to warmed dinner plates, and pour some of the pan juices over each one. Sprinkle with the reserved chopped oregano and serve.

2 Cornish game hens (about 1½ pounds each), butterflied (slit down the breasts and pulled back so the birds lie as flat as possible)

1 bunch fresh oregano sprigs

¼ cup extra-virgin olive oil

Fresh juice of 1 lemon

3 garlic cloves, peeled and thinly sliced

1 teaspoon red pepper flakes, or to taste

Kosher or sea salt, to taste

Butcher's Note: It may have been a snappy marketing tool to call a small, young chicken something as fancy and compelling as a Cornish hen, but it worked. And despite the fact that they have nothing to do with Cornwall, nor are they game, these chickens are quite good and versatile. The full name is Rock Cornish game hens, indicating a cross between Cornish and white Plymouth Rock chickens.

contamination. But if you grind your own meat on the premises, from trim *you* have trimmed, from meat *you* can vouch for, your customer can trust that the condition of your product is the ne plus ultra. Wherever passion, professionalism, dedication, and hands-on attention are found, there is cleanliness. Supermarket chains have long given up on Ray Venezia's primary precept. Their chopped meat comes to them in boxes from God knows what grade of animal, chopped and vacuum-packed God knows how long ago.

The next most important thing for Ray is that the butcher who waits on you must know the right cut of meat for your recipe. Hardly anybody cooks anymore, and almost certainly the guy waiting on you at the supermarket meat and poultry counter doesn't cook. Not so at Ray's Fairway counters. The employees there have specifically demonstrated that they do cook, that they are passionate about knowing the right cut for the recipe at hand. So, obviously, for those of you who desire to purchase the best meats and poultry—and can't get to our operation at Fairway—it is your mission to find an operation which cuts and grinds everything on the premises and whose workers really know their product.

Four Rules for a Serious Burger

Mitchel London is, for all his highfalutin food passions and wanton consumption, a burger freak. It figures that the Mitchel burger would be definitive, if not the best burger of anyone's life, or certainly of *my* life. Mitchel recently opened a shop called Burgers & Cupcakes in Hell's Kitchen, on Ninth Avenue. The interior walls are painted to suggest a cupcake—hideous magenta and brown, like a Dunkin' Donuts. And the name is apt: he serves nothing but burgers, french fries, and cupcakes. Mitchel's cupcakes are drop-dead good, but his burgers and fries are a religious experience, in my opinion.

To us a good crust is a large part of what makes a good burger, and we don't mean the bun. To get a good crust, we use a flat griddle instead of a grill. With a griddle you get the flavor of the meat, not the charcoal, and a predictably good crust if you follow the rules.

We're not didactic about all aspects of burgers, though. For instance, the size of your burger is a personal decision. And there are serious ratio issues regarding the size of the patty and the size of the bun. Some people are proponents of the monster patty with a small bun; some like the sturdy, in-your-face bun with a flat patty and lots of toppings (I suspect these are closet vegetarians). Mitchel and I like burgers to be in direct proportion to their buns, like noses and breasts—not too big and not too small. We're partial to a 6-ounce burger made with a blend of 80 percent meat to 20 percent fat. However, unless you get a butcher (like Ray) to grind it for you fresh, you may have to use your market's ground beef mixture.

The type of bun is also controversial. There are people who love crusty rolls and even people who love pocket pita. Believe it or not, Mitchel and I prefer a traditional, soft, commercial-style burger bun, nothing gourmet (with minimal toppings—maybe some cheese, but not always).

The Rules

1. When making the patty, handle the meat as little as possible. You should treat it as you would a delicate scrambled egg, barely forming it so you retain the crumbly texture of the ground beef and don't end up with a dense, joyless burger.
2. Preheat a heavy pan (well-seasoned cast iron works great), using *no* salt and *no* oil.
3. Once the pan is very hot (and this is crucial), slap the burger on and *don't move it for 4 minutes.* You're trying to get a good crust on the burger. The crust gives the burger a lot of flavor and texture. Now flip the burger and let it sit for another 5 minutes. After a total cooking time of 9 minutes, a 6-ounce burger will be medium-rare. For medium, leave it on another 2 minutes. (If you want it well done, you probably don't really want a burger—do yourself a favor and eat something else.)
4. Do *not* press down on the burger, no matter how many times you've seen people do this in the movies. Pressing down might make the burger cook faster, but it will guarantee a dry, listless piece of meat.

Now slap this beauty on a nice soft roll. A pinch of kosher salt, a nice slice of ripe tomato (if it's August), maybe a slice of red onion (if you don't have a date later), ketchup (if you must), and that's it!

Sautéed Veal Chop with Arugula Salad

Serves 4

A light, fresh, delicious version of the classic veal milanese.

4 boneless veal chops (cutlets), about 1¼ inches thick, pounded to ¼ inch thick

Kosher or sea salt and freshly ground black pepper

4 handfuls baby arugula (about 6 ounces)

4 to 6 tablespoons extra-virgin olive oil, as needed

2 medium tomatoes, seeded and cut into ½-inch dice

½ medium red onion, peeled, halved, and very thinly sliced

Fresh juice of 1 lemon

Corn oil, for sautéing

1. Season both sides of each veal chop with salt and pepper.
2. In a large salad bowl, toss the arugula with 4 tablespoons of the olive oil. In a separate bowl, toss the tomatoes and onion with the lemon juice and salt and pepper to taste.
3. In a large frying pan over medium heat, warm just enough corn oil to coat the bottom of the pan (you'll be sautéing these chops one at a time since they've gotten so wide, and you'll probably use about ¼ cup oil in all). When the oil is hot but not smoking, add one of the veal chops and cook, turning once, until it is beginning to brown and the meat is an opaque white, 1 to 1½ minutes on each side. Transfer the veal to a warmed plate and repeat with the remaining chops (alternatively, you can get two pans going at once to fry the meat in half the time).
4. Toss the arugula with a light sprinkling of salt. Use a slotted spoon or fork to transfer the tomatoes and onions to the arugula and toss well. Place the veal chops on four plates and top each one with a large mound of arugula salad.

Butcher's Note: Veal isn't as popular as it ought to be. It is naturally low in fat, and when veal is cooked at a lower temperature for a longer time, it will result in a knockout of a meal.

I love Ray like the brother I never had. I worry about him, though. He is *so* type A. He's also a megalomaniac. As if running the city's biggest meat and poultry operation weren't enough, Ray has allowed himself to be persuaded to assume the role of "super-GM" of all four Fairways. He is the go-to guy for any matter a store's GM can't handle—or is not handling in a way Ray likes. He also oversees our graphics department, the security guys, the newspaper ads, the cashiers, and the operation of the "front-ends" (checkout). You name it, Ray's probably got his fingers in it. Not to mention that he and his wife and three kids of high school and college age live way out in New Jersey near the Pennsylvania border, so Ray has an hour-plus commute each way six days a week. He may be several years younger than I am, but I couldn't keep up his pace and volume of work. No way. I comfort myself and assuage my guilt by reminding myself that the more work Ray does, the less I have to do.

Ray's hands slicing veal for scalloppine.

4

The Fish Department,

Captain Tony

at the Helm

Fairway has been in the fresh seafood business for only ten years. Early on, we had another fellow and his son doing all the buying and merchandising in our two stores, but we just weren't satisfied with their work, and so we found Tony Maltese. After all, the founders of Fairway—Howie, Harold, and David—are serious, boat-owning fishermen, so you can be sure that when we got into fish and seafood, we'd insist on doing it right.

Tony Maltese was a professional fisherman before he ever got involved in the retail end of seafood. He is my age. Born and raised in Brooklyn. He caught some pretty big tuna in his day, bluefin mostly: 535 pounds, 550 pounds, a whopper of 760 pounds that won him some serious money at a tuna derby off Montauk at the tip of Long Island. He also won a few shark tournaments.

There comes a time when hardworking people realize that physical labor is not getting any easier and in fact is becoming almost impossible. They lose their edge, their desire—not to mention their nimbleness and carefulness. Suddenly the job isn't just painful and exhausting; it's dangerous. When that time came for Tony, he made the only sensible move. He joined Fairway.

Tony knows the seafood business inside and out. Inside, because of all those years he was a fisherman. Outside, because he was deeply involved in retail, having sold his catch direct to innumerable stores in the tri-state area. His passion for seafood, his mantra of freshness, his knowledge, and his hands make him an extraordinary retailer. By "hands" I mean what you do with your product to make people want to put it in their shopping cart. It's fairly rare in the food business. I was blessed with hands—I taught myself how to lay out cheeses and olives and all my other stuff in a fashion that makes it well-nigh impossible to resist making a purchase or two, or three. Our produce buyer Peter Romano—the boss of the backbone of Fairway, fruits and vegetables—was also blessed with a pair of hands. Tony has hands. His counters, to me, are as holy as any altar, and I don't give compliments like that to very many people in this business. To stand and regard the rows and rows of Tony's creatures is, for me, a joy. I've spent a lot of time in seafood-mad cities in Europe, Australia, and elsewhere: cities like Palermo, Nice, Barcelona, Madrid, Sydney, Tunis, Paris, and Brussels. I've stood for uncountable hours in the shops and at the street stands of fishmongers whose entire families, for generations, have been working side by side—families whose reputations have always been defined by the majesty of their work. Glistening, twitching, glowing critters of all shapes and sizes and every taxonomy. Every day Tony's counters are a staggeringly beautiful still life that quickens the blood of even the most jaded New York shopper.

Tony buys fish and seafood only for today—every day of the week, including Sunday. That's because, he says, freshness is everything. Use your nose. Walk up to a fish counter, and if you smell fish, walk away. Tony says a blind man could decide whether or not a fish counter is going to get his busi-

PREVIOUS SPREAD, LEFT:
Fresh smelts—heavenly, whether roasted, grilled, or pan-fried. We devour them with our fingers, like an ear of corn.

Nightmare at Sea

Once Tony was on the receiving end of a real horror story directly related to his profession. Twenty years ago, he was working as the captain of a fishing boat whose owner had asked him to return to a spot about twenty miles off the south shore of Long Island and 100 feet deep, where another of the owner's boats had lost a very expensive fishing net. Scuba diving would be needed to find and retrieve it—something Tony and his crewmates loved doing—so the position had been marked with a buoy. With Tony at the helm, his crewmates swam to the bottom, about seventy-five feet below. It was apparently just pure luck that, so far from shore, the net had gotten detached from its line over a sort of rise or butte on the seafloor. Otherwise the depth of the ocean could have been many hundreds of feet down, far too deep for scuba divers.

Well, surprise, surprise. At the bottom was a sleek, shiny new cabin cruiser that apparently hadn't been down there long. A diver cased out the interior. There were no bodies—but there were lots of big bales of hashish. Tony immediately called the Coast Guard, which immediately dispatched a very scary helicopter manned by skeptical and unappreciative agents of the DEA. From that moment on, for the next five years, Tony's life was a nightmare. Not only was he detained, accused, threatened, and ultimately, outrageously left hanging out to dry by the local Long Island cops and, worse, by the FBI and DEA, but he and his family—his wife and daughter—were squarely in the sights of some mobsters who were certain that Tony had stolen their drugs, and they made it painfully clear that he wasn't going to get away with it. Tony went through absolute terror, fury, and hell before the issue was finally settled. He actually had to arm himself to the teeth, and his home on Long Island became a bunker for months. All because he did the right thing and called in to report what he'd found. Scary.

ness. A seafood counter that displays fish and seafood in a refrigerated case is a warning sign too. The case must be open; the wares must be on ice. This is how a fishmonger demonstrates that his product is as fresh as can be. Is the fish wrapped? Don't buy it. Wrapped fish is old fish.

Variety is an enormous part of why Fairway's seafood operations are so successful, so vital, so talked-about and imitated. Well, imitated to a point. It is the rare retail seafood operation that offers any of the less prominent choices. Tony most loves the stuff he sells the least of—cockles, whelks, razor clams, sardines, oysters, sea urchins—so he keeps bringing it in. At

Rosemary and Chile–Grilled Shrimp with Lemon Zest

Serves 4

This is an extremely delicious and easy way to enjoy shrimp. Leaving the tails on means there's less chance that the shrimp will slip through the grill grate. And they're a perfect finger food. After you've cooked them, you could serve them hot or at room temperature with salad greens (frisée, Boston, whatever) and a vinaigrette, or as a main course with just about anything.

Shrimp are a great blessing in this life. Big shrimp, small shrimp—tigers, all of them. I wish the industry would leave the damn heads on, though. I swear shrimp taste better if they're cooked with their heads on. All that gunk in there is flavor, no doubt about it. But Americans can be so squeamish. God forbid that an American should roast a fish with its head on.

1 pound medium shrimp (24 to 32 shrimp), peeled and deveined, tails left on

½ cup extra-virgin olive oil

Fresh juice and zest of 1 lemon

3 to 4 fresh small red chile peppers, seeded and finely chopped

Leaves from 2 sprigs rosemary, chopped

2 garlic cloves, peeled and finely chopped

Kosher or sea salt to taste

1. In a large bowl, toss the shrimp with the oil, lemon juice, chile peppers, rosemary, garlic, and a pinch of salt. Cover and refrigerate for 30 to 45 minutes.

2. Light the grill or heat a cast-iron frying pan over high heat until very hot. Remove the shrimp from the marinade and grill or sear them until just pink and opaque, about 1 minute per side.

3. Transfer the cooked shrimp to a platter. Sprinkle with the lemon zest and season with salt to taste. Serve immediately.

Fishmonger's Note: Buying shrimp is nearly foolproof. It would be nice to be able to get fresh (never frozen) shrimp, but that's just a pipe dream because lots of fishermen freeze shrimp onboard or at least ice them down so hard they nearly freeze. No matter. Shrimp thaw beautifully the first time around and cook up just about as fresh and sweet as they would be if you boiled them as soon as you caught them.

And Then There Are the Gulf Shrimp

Not everything European is better, I should say.

Nowadays, my mom and dad live on the gulf coast of Alabama. We know from fresh shrimp down there. We get the deepwater red shrimp, the sweetest, most delicious shrimp that swim. They are even better than langoustines—prawn-size lobsters fished off the coasts of Europe and in the Mediterranean. Gulf red shrimp blow away the snobby, unaffordable imported langoustines.

most seafood counters, all you can really be sure of finding is tuna, salmon, shrimp, snapper, sole, and maybe lobsters and mussels. That stuff is just a jumping-off point for Fairway. Tony flies in Hawaiian fish, wild Pacific salmon and halibut from Alaska, lobsters from Maine, mussels from New Zealand. He also gets branzino, the diminutive, delicate, delicious Mediterranean sea bass; dried cod (*bacalao, baccalà, stoccafisso,* etc.) from Portugal; and *percebes,* the exquisite barnacles from the rocky, wave-swept cliffs of Galicia. He gets truckloads of shrimp (heads on) from the Gulf of Mexico. A lot of the fish he gets is farmed, too, because, he says, he has found that it's excellent. He reminds me that the oceans are in danger of being fished out. As if a person could forget.

Tony stresses the simplicity and joy of roasting, steaming, poaching, and pan-frying whole fish—whole fish, not namby-pamby fillets and steaks. Once seafood lovers taste the difference between a pre-apportioned piece of fish and a whole, head-on fish, they never go back. Plus, the price of whole fish is more reasonable than that of fillets and steaks.

I've swooned over lots of seafood in my life. First, of course, for me, a landlocked, seafood-ignorant Missourian, the fish we ate was fish we caught in ponds, lakes, and streams—bluegill, pumpkinseed, sunfish, perch, largemouth and smallmouth bass, trout, catfish. Gutted, scaled, rolled in cornmeal seasoned with salt and pepper, fried in hot corn oil, and served with tartar sauce.

Olive oil? Unheard of. Tuna? I didn't taste fresh tuna until I came to New York in 1973. I'd never even realized that tuna didn't have to come from a can. Where I came from, supermarkets didn't have seafood departments. Heaven was when my mom and dad took us out to the Howard Johnson's on Highway 40 on Tuesday night for all-you-can-eat fried clams. And the truest bliss for me, aside from my mom's and her mom's cooking, which rarely involved seafood, was surf 'n' turf from the restaurant at the Holiday Inn, also out on the highway. Now, you know as well as I that those clam strips and lobster tails had been frozen like a brick for God knows how long. At the time I didn't know and I wouldn't have cared. I loved it.

But how you gonna keep them down on the farm after they've seen Paree? Starting in 1979 I became an habitué of the great seafood restaurants of Paris and the raw oyster bars of Montmartre—I became an unrepentant oyster freak. (A dozen are just a starter for me; I can eat three dozen before my main course.) I am equally crazy about clams; and mussels, too, are a joy. I went to Le Dôme in Montparnasse, Le Bernardin off the Champs-Elysées,

Tony Maltese, Fairway's master fishmonger.

Fennel-Roasted Whole Branzino

Roasted whole fish tastes so much better than a fillet or steak—the fish cooks up moister and more flavorful on the bone. This preparation is a cinch, it's a beautiful presentation, and it makes you realize what you've been missing if you've never done it before (and most people haven't). By the way, if bones bother you, you really just need to get over that. You can fillet the cooked fish before you serve it, but Mitchel and I hope you won't.

Accompaniments are your choice. I love to serve this with a green salad and a perfect, middle-aged goat's milk cheese on the side, with plenty of crusty bread.

2 whole, cleaned branzini (1 to 1½ pounds each)

Kosher or sea salt and freshly ground black pepper, for seasoning

1 fresh fennel bulb, thinly sliced

3 tablespoons extra-virgin olive oil, plus additional for serving

Coarsely chopped flat-leaf parsley, for garnish

1. Preheat the oven to 450°F.
2. Pat the fish dry. Season the cavities and exterior of each fish with salt and pepper.
3. Spread the fennel in the bottom of a cast-iron pan or a shallow, heavy-bottomed oven-to-table baking dish large enough to accommodate the fish. Arrange the fish on top of the fennel and drizzle with the olive oil. Sprinkle each fish with a pinch of salt. Roast until the head can be easily removed with a butter knife, about 25 minutes.
4. Remove the fish from the oven. Divide the roasted fennel between two warmed dinner plates and top with the branzino. Drizzle the fish with a little more olive oil, sprinkle on a little more sea salt, and garnish with parsley.

Fishmonger's Note: Branzino is the Mediterranean sea bass, a delicious fish. It is a perfect size in that one per person is usually just right. You can also substitute any fish of similar size that is served whole, such as striped bass or red snapper.

Gérard Allamandou's La Cagouille, the Minchelli brothers' Le Duc, Restaurant Guy Savoy, and others. In Madrid, I worshipped a number of times at La Trainera, where I learned that frying fish in olive oil is magic, or can be, depending on the magical abilities of the cook.

All over the Côte d'Azur I learned that I liked grilled fresh sardines even better than butter-drenched, summer Missouri corn—and that the method of holding and eating them is practically identical.

In Puglia, on the Adriatic, I learned how to manipulate a pocket knife efficiently so that the gonads of a sea urchin would be perfectly exposed. For

---

STEVE'S BLOG OF THE DAY
September 11, 2006

Just got back from my niece's wedding in Sturgeon Bay, Wisconsin, up in Door County, the peninsula that sticks out into Lake Michigan above Green Bay. It's so pretty up there it hurts. Now, maybe I'm overly impressionable, but this "fish boil" business is wonderful. If you know what I'm referring to, you're probably thinking, "Jesus, what a dope. Fish boils are for tourists." Well, there's a huge wood fire under a huge cauldron filled with lake water boiling away like crazy. A guy drops in a couple of buckets' worth of smallish peeled Spanish onions and potatoes. They cook. He drops in a couple of buckets' worth of fresh, thick whitefish steaks. They cook.

Fire burning hot. Water slopping over the side of the cauldron. Fish deemed done, the guy splashes a big jar of kerosene *right into the fire.* The conflagration shoots up thirty feet high; everybody oohs and ahhs. This is apparently to boil off the oil from the whitefish that's floating on the surface. The guy and a helper guy poke a big stick through the slots on either side of the cauldron and haul it off to be served.

The tradition came from the old steamers, the Great Lakes fishing boats, which all had to have water on board to make the steam that turned the propellers. The fishermen used to cook the whitefish right on board, right out of the vessel that held the boiling water. I'm a sucker for that theatricality and tradition, and I don't care who knows it. But what seals the deal for me is being served onions and potatoes and whitefish steaks with a big ramekin of melted butter and Door County corn, which has the rightful reputation of being absolutely killer.

I accompanied my dinner with Scotch rocks and cold beer. Could've used some Tabasco or Texas Pete or something, though. Nothing more extreme. Those hotter hot sauces like Hiccuppin' Hot Sauce by the Bone Suckin' BBQ sauce people are so fine, but I just can't take them anymore. Not even my fave of all, Busha Browne's Pukka Scotch bonnet hot sauce. It's like a shotgun shell went off in my butt. Who needs that?

Mussels Steamed with White Wine and Shallots

Serves 2

Belgians *own* mussels, but the Ligurians also know what they're doing when it comes to mussels. At least at Portovenere they do. Portovenere is just below the Cinque Terre, as far east as you can go before it's not the Italian Riviera anymore. There are beds of *datteri di mare* (they call mussels "sea dates") everywhere—those stakes sticking up out of the water are a giveaway. All the *trattorie* serve mussels. If you've never been to Portovenere, you have to go one day. Stay at the Hotel Royal Sporting. Every room has a terrace over the water, and there's a saltwater pool about twenty feet deep. Paradise.

2 quarts smallish mussels (see Fishmonger's Note)

1 cup dry white wine

2 shallots, minced

1 sprig thyme

2 sprigs flat-leaf parsley, roughly chopped

Kosher or sea salt and freshly ground black pepper, to taste

Grilled crusty bread slices, for serving

1. Clean the mussels just before cooking by scrubbing them with a brush under cold running water and scraping off any barnacles with a paring knife. If the beard (byssus) is still attached, remove it by pulling it from the tip of the mussel to the hinge and cutting it off with your knife.

2. In a large nonreactive pot (such as stainless steel) over high heat, combine the wine, shallots, thyme, half of the chopped parsley, a pinch of salt, and a little pepper and bring to a boil.

3. Add the mussels and stir once just to mix up the ingredients. Cover the pot with a tight-fitting lid. Holding the lid to the pot with potholders, shake the pot to thoroughly coat the mussels with wine and aromatics. Cook over high heat until the mussels have opened, 5 to 10 minutes. Divide the mussels and their cooking liquid among large individual bowls (if the cooking liquid seems sandy, transfer it to a glass measuring cup and let it settle for a few minutes, then pour carefully, leaving the grit behind). Garnish with the remaining chopped parsley. Serve with the grilled bread.

Fishmonger's Note: Always buy mussels from a trusted fishmonger. Select only pleasantly briny-smelling ones with closed shells and store them in a plastic bag with ice packed around them in the bottommost compartment of the fridge. Don't keep them for more than three days. While cleaning, if you discover an open shell, tap it to see if it closes. If it doesn't, discard it. Likewise, don't try to eat any mussels that did not open while cooking.

you sushi fans who die for *uni*, the glistening, apricot-colored custard that is the epitome of flavor, I think you know what I'm talking about.

I don't care what anybody says. Venice is still a fabulous city for the seafood lover. Even the otherwise bland razor clams taste like heaven there. *Sarde in saor* is a dish of sardines layered with onions, tiny raisins, and red wine vinegar, and I could eat it every day forever. Venetian *mantecato,* perhaps Venice's most famous dish—desalted dried cod whipped up with garlic and olive oil, called *brandade de morue* in the south of France—is a particular passion of mine. We make it in the Fairway kitchen and sell it cold, like a dip. (I import huge cans of pureed salt cod from Sète, west of Marseille.)

Bottarga, dried tuna (or mullet) roe from Sicily, among other places around the Mediterranean, is sold in units that often look exactly like a canoe paddle. They're visually confounding and would seem to be inedible. But cut *bottarga* into paper-thin slices, drizzle it with olive oil and a squeeze of Sicilian lemon, and serve it with some good crusty bread, and, well, it's pretty wonderful. Or grate it and toss it with *spaghetti all'aglio ed olio* . . . oh, my. We sell *bottarga* at Fairway, but not many people are brave enough to try it. They don't know what they're missing.

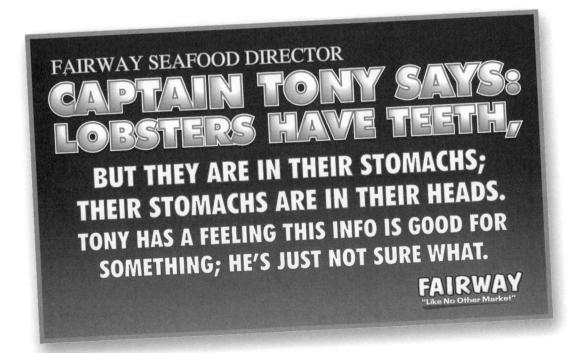

FAIRWAY SEAFOOD DIRECTOR
CAPTAIN TONY SAYS:
LOBSTERS HAVE TEETH,
BUT THEY ARE IN THEIR STOMACHS;
THEIR STOMACHS ARE IN THEIR HEADS.
TONY HAS A FEELING THIS INFO IS GOOD FOR
SOMETHING; HE'S JUST NOT SURE WHAT.

FAIRWAY
"Like No Other Market"

5

The Deli and Appetizing Counter:
A Grand Old New York Tradition

Having been a Missourian for twenty-three years and a New Yorker for thirty-four, I am qualified to inform you that the single biggest thing distinguishing New York from everywhere else in the United States is the New York deli and the appetizing counter. Operators of so-called delicatessens in other cities may think they have it all, but they're either neophytes or just plain lying.

First, the deli counter. At all four Fairways we offer a huge variety of kitchen-prepared foods, sides, and mains, in bulk. Most of it is prepared by people supervised by John Rossi and Mitchel London, and most of the recipes are Mitchel's. As you might imagine, I'm rather proud of the prepared foods we turn out. I taste or serve everything we make every week. Across from the counters, we have refrigerated display cases with several shelves—we call those units "multidecks"—that offer even more kitchen-prepared mains and sides, including quarts of soups, broths, chili, sandwiches, shepherd's pies, quiches, potpies, rotisserie chicken, guacamole, vinaigrettes, Indian foods, Japanese foods, pasta sauces, and fresh pasta. We have hot-food tables, pizza ovens, salad bars, sushi counters. We have pretty much everything anybody could possibly want to eat.

But that's not a complete deli counter. There must also be smoked and cured meats and fish. Delicatessens are an eastern European Jewish phenomenon, and the best of them were brought to western Europe in the eighteenth century and to the New World by the beginning of the twentieth century. As the operators became less strict about foodstuffs Jews deem *trayf* (forbidden), delis evolved to become what the French call *charcuteries* and the Italians call *salumerie*—both terms that refer to cooked, cured, or smoked meats and fish, particularly meats. Smoked fish, especially smoked salmon, always seemed to reside at another counter, the "appetizing" counter, as far away from any pork as possible.

So a proper deli counter—or *charcuterie* or *salumeria*—must offer a number of specific meats. Salami, whether kosher or not, must be there in abundance. For any of you who have never tasted artisanal pork, salami made by hand by artisan specialists in the French regions Lyonnais, Ardèche, Savoie, Burgundy, and others—well, I just cannot overemphasize that this boy's food life just would not have happened without such salami. Serious *saucisson sec* (French for salami) really made the lights of gastronomy go on for me. Italy, too, of course, produces salami that are a religious experience; they come from every region in Italy, certainly Umbria, Tuscany, Abruzzi, Sardinia, and Sicily. Spain's *salchichón* and chorizo are worshipped every bit as much as Italian and French cured or smoked pork products.

We can get Italian mortadella, the only real bologna. (Mortadella was named for the mortar and pestle once used to pound the pork mixture, to which pork fat and pistachios would be added before baking. It originated in the capital of Emilia-Romagna, Bologna—hence the name, which most of

New York Deli–Style Roast Beef Sandwich with Coleslaw and Russian Dressing

Serves 4 to 6

Few things on the face of the earth make me happier than a proper roast beef sandwich, and Mitchel is obsessive—fanatical—about this sandwich. His is a stacked-high wonder of bloody, freshly roasted beef; sweet, crunchy deli coleslaw; and creamy Russian dressing with pickle relish and tangy little slices of cornichons. In other words: this sandwich is a meal. In this recipe, Mitchel has you roast the beef for the sandwiches, but of course you can always go to a good deli and buy meat—just make sure it is very rare and very thinly sliced.

1. Preheat the oven to 450°F. Rub the steaks all over with kosher salt (about ½ teaspoon per steak). Place the steaks on a rimmed baking sheet and roast until the meat registers 130°F on an instant-read thermometer, about 25 minutes. Transfer to a board and let rest until cool (about 30 minutes). If possible, don't refrigerate the meat before assembling the sandwiches.

2. For the slaw, in a large bowl whisk together the mayonnaise, sugar, and vinegar. Add the cabbage and carrot and toss well, then season with salt and pepper.

3. Fold together all the ingredients for the Russian dressing.

4. Slice the beef very thinly against the grain. To assemble, spread Russian dressing on one side of each slice of rye bread. Divide the sliced beef among half the slices of bread. For a deli-style look, drape the meat in a mound rather than laying it flat. Sprinkle the meat with a little salt, then top each sandwich with a generous scoop of coleslaw. Top the slaw with another small dollop of Russian dressing, close the sandwiches, and slice them in half. Provide plenty of napkins for your guests. (If your sandwich isn't a little messy, you did something wrong.)

ROAST BEEF:

3 shell steaks (about ¾ pound each)
Kosher salt

COLESLAW:

¾ to 1 cup mayonnaise

¼ cup sugar

2 tablespoons cider vinegar

½ head green cabbage, cored and finely shredded

1 carrot, peeled and coarsely grated

Kosher or sea salt and freshly ground black pepper, to taste

RUSSIAN DRESSING:

½ cup mayonnaise

¼ cup ketchup

¼ cup sweet pickle relish, drained well in a sieve

3 cornichons, thinly sliced

FOR SERVING:

8 to 12 slices seeded Jewish rye

Kosher salt

Butcher's Note: Mitchel calls for strip loin, which is a shell steak. You could also use roast porterhouse. The porterhouse, it is said (among other stories), was named for a bygone restaurant downtown on Pearl Street in the Manhattan financial district called Porter House. It served a "house" cut consisting of the shell on top and the fillet on the bottom. Keep porterhouse in mind as an option if you can't find strip loin. Otherwise, do what Mitchel tells you to do; he's made a lot of these sandwiches.

us pronounce "baloney.") And we can also get the three great prosciuttos (in Italian, *prosciutti*): air-dried, salt-cured, preservative-free hams. The first is, of course, the famous prosciutto di Parma, another important city in Emilia-Romagna, as well as the identical product from its sister city, Langhirano. Then there are the hams from Friuli-Venezia Giulia, the region above Venice, which are every bit as good as the ones from Parma and Langhirano; differences are opinion and conjecture. Finally, there are the *prosciutti* of Carpegna and San Leo, both towns in the Marches, the Italian region on the Adriatic.

Prosciutto is a way of life in Italy. It is meant to be sliced paper-thin—and enjoyed in its entirety. This means that anybody who removes the ring of fat encircling the lean is a fool. I have a sign posted at each Fairway deli counter that patiently explains this, and closes with a warning that if you insist that your deli person remove it, you are likely to be ignored or insulted. Or both.

ABOUT PROSCIUTTO

That creamy ribbon of fat around the lean part of every prosciutto ham is every bit as important to the enjoyment of this majestic meat as is the lean part. It is the fat that brings out prosciutto's flavor. No prosciutto-loving Italian would allow it to be trimmed away. It would be unthinkable. Please do not ask your counterman to trim it away. He has been trained not to, if it bothers you trim it away at home, but know that you are throwing away prosciutto's flavor, not to mention committing a cardinal gastronomic faux pas.

FAIRWAY
"Like No Other Market"

So we can stock imported Italian prosciutto and mortadella. We can stock *Bundnerfleisch,* the famous air-dried beef from the Grisons canton of Switzerland. The *Bundnerfleisch* is sliced paper-thin into a gorgeous reddish-purplish rectangle—fan it out on a platter or plate; strew it with arugula, a crumble of a goat's milk cheese, a few peeled sections of grapefruit, a splash of some very old balsamic vinegar, and a drizzle of olive oil; give the whole thing a liberal twist of the pepper mill; and you have a lovely repast. And then there is the rest of it. Westphalian ham, smoky and salty, from Germany (legal); and Black Forest ham, not so smoky or salty, also from Germany (legal). You can add to that the domestic production of hams and salami, as well as domestic pâtés and terrines of pork and pork liver, chicken liver, pheasant, and wild boar.

To move on: There are many fine domestic brands that produce standard pâtés, including D'Artagnan, Les Trois Petites Cochons, Marcel et Henri, Alexia, and others. Some of these are coarse-textured, as is a classic pâté maison or pâté de campagne (country-style); some are creamy, mousse-like, as is a chicken liver pâté . . . which brings us to the traditional Jewish deli, where chopped chicken liver is de rigueur. There are few things I love more than chopped liver.

Observant Jews who keep kosher do not mix meat and dairy products. This is just one of many ancient dietary laws that are far too arcane to discuss here, despite the fact that I find them fascinating. In any case, Jewish-style appetizing, referred to in the biz as appy, was devised by Jews who kept kosher. It is considered "dairy," meaning foods that are OK to eat along with dairy products. There really aren't many actual dairy products to be found at the appetizing counter, other than herring in cream sauce and cream cheese. But that's OK; those are enough—they're indispensable, in fact.

The essence of appetizing is smoked fish, along with its traditional accompaniments—pickled tomatoes, kosher dill and half-sour Kirby cucum-

Artisanal American Charcuterie

I am ecstatic to report that Americans are finally taking the notion of charcuterie and *salumi* seriously. A growing number of artisans are crafting wonderful cured and smoked meats and fish. We have several rare-breed hams—hardwood-smoked, netted hams—that are beyond delicious. We slice them for customers right off the bone. There is a salami and mortadella maker named Paul Bertolli from Berkeley, California, whose stuff (Fra'Mani brand) is as good as or better than anything I've tasted in Europe. Tom Pacicca's applewood-smoked trout comes to us still warm from the smoker. Herb Eckhouse's Iowa prosciutto ranks with the best in the world. His company is called La Quercia, the Italian word for "oak tree," in reference to the preferred diet (acorns) of the hogs that make the best *salumi*, whether in Europe or the United States. Herb also sends us *guanciale* ("gwan-CHA-leh"), the cured, fatty jowl of his hogs, a *salumi* item held in high esteem in parts of Italy. In Rome, for example, *guanciale* is the prime ingredient in *spaghetti all'amatriciana,* a dish similar to, though distinctly separate from, *spaghetti alla carbonara*—"charcoal-maker's" pasta—for which pancetta is used instead of *guanciale.*

bers, herring in its myriad forms (the aforementioned cream sauce with onions is the standard, though *matjes*, meaning "maiden," or young, herring is also popular), seeded rye bread and butter, borscht, and the like.

Rarely does a purchase at the appetizing counter fail to include lox or smoked salmon—or both. You thought they were the same thing? Not so. True, they are both salmon. The term "lox" comes from the Yiddish *laks* and German *Lachs*, which mean "salmon." But in the business and culture of Jewish-style appetizing, so much a part of so many New Yorkers' upbringing and way of life, *lox* refers to brine-cured, that is, pickled salmon—it isn't smoked. And although smoked salmon is sometimes served to accompany bagels and cream cheese, along with other "appetizing" fare, this is a relatively recent occurrence. My guess is that it was a post–World War II phenomenon, that smoking salmon and other fish such as Great Lakes whitefish, chub, sable (black cod), and sturgeon emerged as a result of demand from eastern European immigrants, among whom a liking for this type of food is ingrained.

Many people, Jewish or not, consider the presence of smoked salmon on the appetizing table odd and extravagant, since tradition calls for lox. Smoked salmon has always been an upper-class, Eurocentric foodstuff, served on plates with lemon and capers and some type of bread on the side. It's meant to be eaten with a knife and fork like a first course or an entrée. In contrast, lox is decidedly down-market fare. The snob factor is present in every food culture, including this one. Still, for gentiles like me, to whom Jewish-style appetizing was foreign until I moved to New York, smoked salmon seemed a natural accompaniment to bagels and cream cheese. And these days plenty of people seem to agree.

Smoked salmon—that is, the European-cum-Jewish New Yorker smoked salmon—is strictly cold-smoked. Cold smoking is the gold standard, in my opinion. The silky, oily, smoky sides of salmon can be sliced by the counterman, who prides himself on his ability to deliver slices thin enough to read through. Out in the country (to a New Yorker, anywhere on the continent other than New York is "out in the country" or "out west"), salmon is "hot-smoked," a method of letting the smoke do its job along with heat. The difference between cold-smoked and hot-smoked salmon is stark. Hot-smoked salmon yields chunks, not slices, of dryish, smoky cooked fish. The smoking boxes that perform these duties differ only in that cold-smoked salmon is kept well away from the source of heat—it's just close enough to absorb the smoke. Both types of smoking boxes use hardwood chips (such as oak, maple, ash, or beech) or fruitwood chips (say, apple or cherry).

Gravlax (or gravlaks) is one of my favorite appetizing foods. Though it is not born of Jewish culture—it's Scandinavian—it has over time been

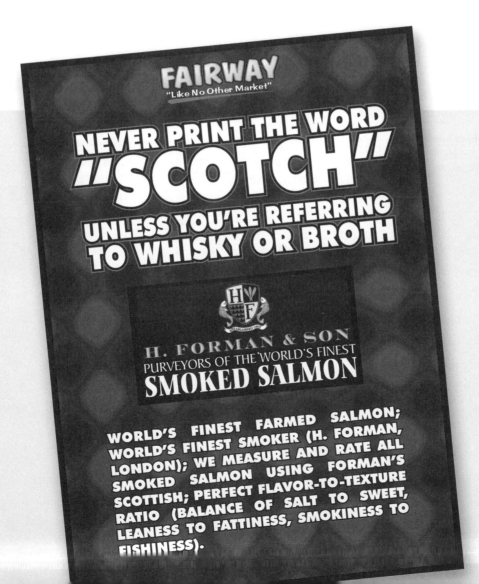

Lox, Eggs, and Onions

Serves 2

Lox is like a forgotten old aunt who used to be beloved and prominent in the life of the family but now is merely tolerated, when she shows up at the house at all. For quite a few years, lox has been sold only at old, established appetizing shops. There are several reasons for this, most of which have to do with the fact that the taste of smoked salmon is more popular, and it's much more widely available than it was before it became a household staple (sometime in the 1980s, wasn't it?).

2 tablespoons corn oil

1 large onion, peeled and chopped (about 2 cups)

4 large eggs

2 tablespoons unsalted butter

5 slices lox (about 4 ounces total), each slice cut crosswise into thirds

4 tablespoons chopped scallions (3 to 4 scallions)

1 teaspoon chopped fresh chives

Kosher salt

1. In a large, heavy skillet over high heat, warm the corn oil. Add the onion and cook, stirring once or twice, until the pieces begin to char and blacken at the ends (charring the onion gives this dish a lot of its flavor), 4 to 5 minutes. Transfer the onion to a sieve set over a bowl to drain.
2. Break the eggs into a mixing bowl and whisk with a fork until just combined.
3. In a large, preferably nonstick pan over medium heat, melt the butter. Add the salmon, separating the pieces, and toss once to coat them with butter. Add the drained charred onion and toss again. Pour the eggs into the pan and let sit for 10 seconds so they start to set. With a wooden spoon, slowly move the eggs around, gently combining them with the lox and onion. *Do not scramble.* Stir in the chopped scallions, then divide the eggs onto warmed plates. Garnish with chopped chives and season to taste with kosher salt.

Chef's Note: A milder smoked salmon such as nova (the least salty smoked salmon available) can be used in this dish, but the saltier, gutsier lox is traditional and provides a sharper contrast with the delicate flavor of the eggs and the sweetness of the onions.

Vanilla-Coconut Macaroons with Chocolate Variation

Makes 18 to 20 macaroons

There are the beloved French macaroons, usually based on almonds and meringue. Then there are coconut macaroons. We import from Flanders a brilliant, chewy coconut macaroon that has devoted fans among Fairway's shoppers. But the Jewish deli macaroon— big, scrumptious, mostly coconut, and sweet enough to wake you up from a stupor induced by bagels and lox—is its own beast. Not only are these macaroons indispensable; they're also about the easiest cookie you could bake. And they're kosher for Passover.

1. Preheat the oven to 350°F. Line two large cookie sheets with parchment paper or nonstick baking liners.
2. In a medium mixing bowl, combine the coconut, sugar, egg whites, vanilla, and salt. Using a rubber spatula, fold the ingredients together until evenly combined.
3. With damp hands (to prevent the cookies from sticking), form cone-shaped cookies, using about 2 tablespoons of batter for each. Place the cookies 1 inch apart on the prepared baking sheets.
4. Bake until the macaroons are light golden-brown, just firm to the touch, and still soft in the center, 15 to 20 minutes.
5. Let the cookies rest on the baking sheets until they are cool enough to handle, about 10 minutes. Transfer them to a wire rack to cool thoroughly.

2½ cups (4 ounces) unsweetened shredded coconut

¾ cup sugar

2 large egg whites

1 teaspoon pure vanilla extract

¼ teaspoon kosher salt

Variation: *Chocolate-Coconut Macaroons.* In a double boiler or metal bowl suspended over, not in, barely simmering water, melt 4 ounces chopped semisweet chocolate (or use semisweet chips), stirring until smooth. Let cool slightly. Meanwhile, make the macaroon batter as for Vanilla-Coconut Macaroons through step 2, adding ¼ cup sifted unsweetened cocoa powder and an additional egg white. Fold the cooled melted chocolate into the macaroon batter, then proceed as for Vanilla-Coconut Macaroons.

Chef's Note: These macaroons are even better when dipped in melted semisweet chocolate. Melt chocolate in a double boiler (or in a small bowl set over a saucepan of simmering water over low heat), stirring until smooth. Dip the pointed end of the cooled macaroon into the melted chocolate so that it is half-immersed. Swirl the macaroon when pulling it out of the chocolate to minimize dripping; then return it to the baking sheet, chocolate-dipped end up, so that the chocolate can harden.

adopted. It is cured salmon, too, though it's not at all like lox, which is fishy-tasting and salty. Gravlax was a Norse means of preserving salmon when there was a glut. The fish were gutted, split into sides, heavily salted and sugared, and then actually buried in the ground, where they would cure. (The word "gravlax" essentially means "buried salmon"—buried as in a grave.) In the modern method, sides or chunks of raw salmon are liberally rubbed with salt, sugar, and fresh dill, then refrigerated and placed under weights, such as heavy platters or bricks, for a period of time (days) until the salmon has cured. The weight on the salmon encourages the cure to "take." When ready, the gravlax is served sliced very thin and accompanied by the traditional mustard-dill sauce, as well as rye bread, black bread, or pumpernickel, and some spiritous beverage. My mouth waters at the mere suggestion.

All our smoked salmon, sable, and sturgeon is sliced by hand at the counter, and slicing is a skill to be prized, in that it can't really be taught. It must be learned by someone who has the ability to wield a knife and the desire to be really proficient. It requires practice, repetition, and patience. I remember how nervous I was back in, oh, 1989, when I decided I had to be able to say that no one slices salmon better than I do. I hacked up quite a few sides of salmon, I freely admit. But once you get the hang of slicing, you realize how manifestly satisfying it is to be able to lift a long, wide, gossamer-thin sheet of sunset-colored flesh from a side of smoked salmon and deftly deposit it on a sheet of "wet" (oil-impervious) wax paper without a wrinkle. For cold-smoking, each salmon is split in two from head to tail. After having been cold-smoked, these sides must be expertly trimmed of their fins and of the gristly edges; and all the pesky pinbones, each around an inch or two long, must be extracted with tweezers. If you try to slice a side of salmon with the pinbones still in it, you are sunk. The salmon will tear.

OPPOSITE:
This is the Fairway deli counter at Broadway and 74th Street in Manhattan.

The most amazing thing I discovered about slicing salmon is how soft your hands become, especially if you slice a lot of it, day after day, for weeks and months. Your hands are as soft as a baby's bottom. Sure, after a day at the appy counter your hands will smell fishy, but that's no big deal. Just rub lemon juice all over them—the way Susan Sarandon did in *Atlantic City*.

AMERICAN PADDLEFISH ROE

1. **VISUALLY SCRUMPTIOUS**
GLISTENS, SPARKLES.

2. **TEXTURALLY PERFECT**
CRISPY, SNAPPY

3. **ABSOLUTELY DELICIOUS**
ELEGANT, LINGERING AFTERTASTE

4. **PLENTIFUL**
CASPIAN STURGEON ARE VIRTUALLY EXTINCT.

5. **AFFORDABLE**

FAIRWAY
"Like No Other Market"

6. **IT'S CAVIAR**
SALMON ROE, LUMPFISH ROE, CAPELIN ROE, WHITEFISH ROE, ETC. ARE NOT <u>CAVIAR!</u>

Except she wasn't rubbing lemon juice on just her hands, as I recall. As if I didn't recall. Hubba hubba.

Sable and sturgeon are much less difficult to slice. Whereas smoked salmon is a horizontal affair requiring concentration, they are sliced at a forty-five-degree angle, yielding compact, thickish slices. Wayman, Vic, and Oscar at the Broadway store; Attol and Ardie up at the Harlem store; Jai Paul out on Long Island at the Plainview Fairway; and Virgil, Ernest, Danny, and Henry at the Red Hook, Brooklyn, store—all these men are superb salmon slicers. They've all been with us for a long time, and we are honored by that fact.

In addition to all the various preparations of salmon found at the Fairway appetizing counter—and sable (smoked, paprika-coated black cod), smoked sturgeon, smoked whitefish, and smoked chub (small Great Lakes whitefish)—we stock smoked tuna, salmon roe, chopped herring, whitefish salad (a passion of mine, particularly served on one of those doughy onion egg rolls), pickled herring fillets, smoked trout, and all kinds of expensive fresh sturgeon caviar from Russia, Iran, the United States (farmed), and other places.

Add to all this scrumptious appetizing food the peerless Fairway bagel in all its variety, our rye bread, our bialy (a traditional flat, hole-less, minced onion–spiked, bagel-like thing—great toasted!), our innumerable cream cheese and tofu spreads, our kosher dill and half-sour pickles, our carrot and raisin salad, our roasted artichoke hearts, our *boquerones* (Catalan Mediterranean anchovies pickled in wine vinegar), our matzo ball soup. . . . Sounds like a deal.

6

Fairway Branches Out:
Three Bold New Stores

The flagship store on Broadway at 74th Street has grown mightily from its original 3,000 square feet to its now sprawling 32,500 square feet, including the upstairs, with its organic department as well as our Fairway Café and Steakhouse. We accomplished this starting in the late 1980s and early 1990s by taking over a dress shop, and not long after, the coffee shop next to us. This extended the store all the way to 74th Street. In the mid-1990s, we made our move into what was an ordinary supermarket directly next door to us to the north, a D'Agostino. Howie, Harold, and David owned that old two-story building, and had to wait until the lease ran out to bring Fairway into the realm of world-class food halls by virtue of a full-service butcher department as well as a full-service seafood operation in addition to aisles of standard groceries. Above the

D'Agostino was a Jack LaLanne gym. There we chose to enter the world of organic fruits and vegetables, organic groceries, and organic dairy products as well as vitamins, supplements, and lots of other organic and all-natural stuff such as soap and health-care products. The sum total is an utter and perpetual riot of activity. What a great and amazing store!

In 1995 we really took a gamble. David, Harold, and Howie bought a store in Harlem at 133rd Street and 12th Avenue, right on the Hudson River at the bottom of the 125th Street exit ramp off the Henry Hudson Parkway. This store was a moribund meat and poultry operation complete with a 10,000-square-foot cold room on the selling floor, a room still kept permanently at about 40 degrees Fahrenheit, where our customers are lent quilted jackets in order not to freeze to death while shopping for meat and poultry. The facility included two floors above the retail store, where sides of beef and boxes of poultry were prepared for retail sale. Back in the 1940s this store would unload entire sides of beef directly from the train tracks, where boxcars would roll off the main line onto a spur. The sides of beef would be attached to hooks hanging from a rail that would allow them to be pushed right into the building

and then up a floor or two, where they were "butchered" for retail. Through the 1980s this store continued to specialize in low prices on meat and poultry, but at that time Harlem had yet to break out of its long depression. Gentrification was a long way off and not yet in sight. But by 1995, Harold and David and Howie could feel a big change coming, and they boldly took up the challenge to do something special.

This part of Harlem was particularly forbidding. Dark, dirty, scary. The television networks' cop shows—like *NYPD Blue* and *Law and Order*—always seemed

Stargazing

Every time I visit my family, I'm asked if I've seen anybody famous at work. After all, this is New York City. And, really, 99 percent of the time, famous people are given space here. Most of us are cool about celebrities. But a few times I have been embarrassed by an idiot worker who says, *"Wow*—Larry Storch! How are you, man?" Cicely Tyson was particularly put out one evening when a cashier blew her cover. These are some of the shiny folks I can remember seeing numerous times at Fairway over the years. Probably there are lots more, but who can remember (or recognize) them all?

The architect I. M. Pei, director Woody Allen, actress Mia Farrow, violinists Itzhak Perlman and Nadja Salerno-Sonnenberg, singer-songwriter Elvis Costello, Redskins and Jets running back John Riggins, trumpeter Wynton Marsalis, saxophonist Joe Temperley, actress Frances McDormand and her director husband, Joel Coen, actor Larry Storch (of *F Troop*), actor Fritz Weaver, actress Barbara Barrie, Broadway star Bernadette Peters, former mayor Ed Koch, former arbitrageur Ivan Boesky, broadcaster Bryant Gumbel, actor Joel Grey and his actress daughter Jennifer Grey, congressman Charles Rangel, restaurateur George Lang, food critic Craig Claiborne, chef Pierre Franey, food critic Gael Greene, actress Sigourney Weaver, actor Laurence ("don't call me Larry!") Fishburne, actor Alec Baldwin, actress Kim Basinger, food critic Mimi Sheraton, graphic artist Milton Glaser, actor Kevin Bacon, tenor Franco Corelli, former Mets slugger Keith Hernandez, Knicks superstar Walt Frazier, Glenn Close, John Sayles (director), Dianne Wiest and Tim Blake Nelson (actors), actors Steve Buschemi and Julia Stiles, playwright Edward Albee . . .

I can't believe I waited on the choreographer George Balanchine so many times. He often bought farmer cheese for *palacsinta*. Probably the rudest and dumbest famous person I ever had the displeasure of waiting on was—wait! That was at Dean & DeLuca. Figures. She's not smart enough to shop at Fairway. What a dope! Joel Grey is a peach.

to be shooting there. Major motion pictures, too. I've seen George Clooney, Richard Gere, and other famous actors on shoots here numerous times, at all hours of the day and night. The piece of real estate that is now the famous Fairway Harlem lies under—literally under—not just the Henry Hudson Parkway and the parallel elevated Amtrak line (on its way to Montreal from Penn Station), but also the viaduct of Riverside Drive, with its vaulting steel arches and massive iron stanchions and abutments. This is a gorgeous piece of en-

gineering and architecture for those of us whose blood rushes at the sight of 100-year-old urban infrastructure. The viaduct starts at about Riverside Church, on 120th Street, and runs north to about 135th Street. It was built above a valley on the Hudson whose center is at the western end of 125th Street, where the Hudson River stretches two miles across to New Jersey. In the earliest days of New York City, it was thought that this valley would serve as the locus of the metropolis. After all, it was a natural deepwater port, a place where all commerce could have been centered. But as it turned out, the locus of the metropolis was downtown at the Battery, and Harlem was left to its own devices.

The Harlem Fairway, starting in December 1995, served as a stimulus for the transformation of an entire neighborhood. West Harlem is hot these days—beyond hot. Real estate prices have gone through the roof as people from all over have flocked to this lovely area, its wonderful buildings, and its very own, now famous agora, a marketplace where great foodstuffs are celebrated every day. It is amazing what a wonderful food store will do for a community. Columbia University—with its enormous portfolio of real estate holdings in the area, a stunning quantity of long-held, mixed-use, and dormant buildings—has long been poised to maximize a vision of theaters, apartments, community centers, dorms, classrooms, and restaurants. Already the neighborhood is buzzing with commercial activity, and Columbia hasn't even gotten started.

It was at the Harlem store that we began to do everything ourselves. We bake the best bagels of your life (kosher, of course) in an ancient, massive oven that rotates trays of

FAIRWAY
"Like No Other Market"

GREAT COFFEE
THE " FAIRWAY BLEND"-- COLOMBIAN & BRAZILIAN ARABICAS; A MEDIUM ROAST,
YET BOLD, FULL, SATISFYING, RICH AND DELICIOUS-- PERFECT COFFEE

TERRIFIC PRICE
TYPICAL; THIS IS FAIRWAY

HANDSOME CAN
JUST WHAT YOU'VE BEEN LOOKING FOR

$2.99
13 OZ CAN

THE FOOD LIFE

Master roaster Richard Pascale, a Fairway superstar.

dough—boiled in city tap water—through it like a Ferris wheel. Angelo Villa-reale, our master baker (we have to say that succinctly), takes pride in his bagels, as he should. His baguettes are getting better and better too. Humid days are a killer for baguettes, though, no matter *who* the baker is.

Our longtime employee and master coffee roaster Richard Pascale—he was "invented" by David Sneddon—first began to roast carefully sourced green (raw) coffee beans in an astronomically expensive German-built coffee roaster that we "flew" above the selling floor. We used to smoke our fish in Harlem; the operation has since moved to Red Hook. Our smoked salmon was recently named in a survey conducted by *New York* magazine as the city's absolute best. (Smoked salmon to New Yorkers is cardinal, cru-cial—it's in our DNA.) We pump a dozen specific olive oils and a balsamic vinegar from barrels into bottles, too.

Our sprawling operation in Harlem includes not just the retail store but the buildings on either side of it. We warehouse and distribute grocer-ies, cheeses, cured meats, and produce to the other stores. One entire red-brick building, vacant for decades, over 100 years old, is now emblazoned

Avanelle Rivera

Is this a great country, or what? This kid was born and raised in Guyana, about as obscure a place as there is, and came with her parents to the United States—Queens, New York, to be exact—in 1975, when she was eleven. Well, she fell into the normal immigrant scheme of things, went to junior high and high school, graduated with a bachelor's degree from one of the area's vocational tech schools, and worked at a few jobs until she was hired by Fairway in the mid-1980s as a counter person in the cheese department. She worked hard and smart; she was dependable, reliable, and easy to work with; the customers loved her; her coworkers loved her; I loved her. After a couple of years, she found herself promoted to manager, then buyer.

Now, she presides over perhaps the most successful and glorious cheese and specialty food operations anywhere in the world. She buys not just cheese from every country that produces it, but the uncountable other high-end foodstuffs that make Fairway what it is. I recently got her certified as a veritable French *maître-fromager:* a master cheesemonger, like me. I suppose the reason she is so successful is the same reason I haven't done too badly—she has a passion for her medium. That makes all the difference.

Avanelle hates the limelight. She is as modest as can be. She'll be traveling with me to Cologne, Germany, in a few weeks to attend the world's largest food industry trade show. Not many American retailers go to the trouble to do this sort of thing. We do—because if we don't, we just won't be acquainted with what's out there.

with stunning hand-painted murals, fanciful impressions of Fairway and the Harlem neighborhood, by Floyd Simmons, the brother of my right-hand woman and master cheesemonger, Avanelle Rivera—Floyd and Avanelle were born and raised in Guyana, by the way. The Harlem store is adjacent to our corporate office.

I spent four solid years at this store, from January 1996 to January 2000, before I began to spend the majority of my time at the Broadway store again. My wife and children and I live in the neighborhood. I walk to work at the Harlem store, a lovely stroll. I walk to the Broadway store, too—I've done it often. But nowadays I like to take the bus so I can read the sports section before I get to work.

A couple of years went by, everything was hunky-dory, and David, Howie, and Harold were offered a turnkey piece of real estate way the hell out on Long Island, in a community called Plainview. It was a defunct supermarket that had gone belly-up. All we had to do, so we thought, was turn that key, load it up with merch, and stand aside. Little did we know that this no-brainer would turn into an enormous effort, an enormous expense, and for a while the greatest professional challenge of our lives. Long Islanders, it turns out, are notoriously difficult, diffident, fickle, and tough nuts to crack. But, by golly, we did it. It took us a couple of years to figure them out, but we seem to have gotten to them. This huge store is now the highest-volume store on Long Island. Long Islanders drive for miles on the infuriating Long Island Expressway and other local highways just to shop at Fairway.

Poached Chicken and Mitchel's Chicken Salad

Makes about 4 quarts stock and about 3 cups chicken breast meat

This is, in my opinion, some of the most tender, delicious chicken out there and is the best starting point for making a variety of chicken salads (see recipes below). The stock is the perfect basis for innumerable soups.

Poached Chicken and Light Chicken Stock

2 whole chickens, weighing 3 to 3½ pounds each

3 carrots, unpeeled, cleaned and roughly chopped

3 celery stalks, including green tops, cleaned and roughly chopped

2 Spanish onions, roughly chopped

2 leeks, cleaned and roughly chopped

1 bunch flat-leaf parsley, stems only, roughly chopped (the leaves won't hurt, but you don't need them and you can use them for other things)

1 bay leaf

5 black peppercorns

1. Place the chickens in a large stockpot and add cold water to cover them by 2 inches (about 4 quarts). Bring to a boil. Once the water boils, lower the heat and keep the pot at a slow simmer. (No big bubbles! If you are having trouble keeping the simmering consistently slow, carefully slide the pot partially off the burner.)

2. Start skimming the foam that rises to the surface. Keep skimming for 10 minutes and then add the remaining ingredients. Continue simmering for 1 hour, occasionally skimming the foam and fat that rise to the top of the stock.

3. Remove the chickens from the pot and let them cool.

4. With your fingers (there's really no other way—for this part, I wear latex gloves, available at the Broadway Fairway, aisle 9) pull all the meat from the carcasses, taking care not to shred it too much. Try to leave the lobes of the chicken breasts intact. To finish the broth, return the carcasses and any extra dark meat (I use only breast meat for my poached chicken salads) to the pot and continue to simmer the broth for another hour. Strain the broth, cool it completely, and store it covered in the refrigerator for up to 3 days or freeze it for up to a month.

Chef's Note: As with most things, this poached chicken is best if used in soup, salads, or sandwiches right away, before it is refrigerated.

Traditional Chicken Salad, with Tarragon Variation

At first glance, this recipe looks almost too easy. When I saw it, I said to Mitchel, "Don't you think your recipe is too simplistic to bother telling people about it? I mean, aren't readers going to look at this and say wha-a-a?"

Mitchel gives me a look that says I am the idiot of the day, turns on his heel, stomps off, and returns in about twenty minutes with a plate piled high with this chicken salad, warm and fragrant. He demands that I taste it. I taste it. I have never encountered another chicken salad remotely as good as this one.

I should have known never to second-guess Mitchel. This is a simple recipe, but if it's made with delicate poached chicken, there's none better. If you like tarragon (people seem to either love it or hate it—I love it), try the variation. Remember, a little fresh tarragon goes a long way. Either variation is enough for 2 people.

In a bowl, combine 1½ cups poached, shredded white chicken meat (the meat from 1 large chicken breast) with ¼ cup mayonnaise, 2 small finely diced celery stalks, and salt and pepper to taste.

To make Tarragon Chicken Salad, replace the celery with 1 tablespoon roughly chopped fresh tarragon leaves.

Chef's Note: My favorite traditional chicken salad sandwich is made on Eli's seven-grain bread with raw watercress. My favorite tarragon chicken salad sandwich is made on toasted brioche bread with baby arugula. Whichever one you opt for, don't forget to spread a little mayo on the bread before assembling the sandwich!

And even then it wasn't enough. David, Howie, and Harold wanted more. They got wind of what might be the most dramatic piece of real estate in New York, a pre–Civil War brick warehouse right on the water out in Red Hook, Brooklyn, with five floors and numerous huge cathedral windows, each with black iron shutters. When this warehouse was built, cargo-laden sailing ships delivered coffee and cotton. The ships hauled in and tied up right there in front of our building. Stevedores winched and pulleyed stuff out of the holds and dropped it onto the dock, whereupon each load was hooked to a rope attached to one of the pulleys bolted above every window. The rope was harnessed to a mule that was inside the building, and the mule powered the goods up to whichever of the top four floors was going to house the bales or whatever.

The top three floors of the five-story building are no longer a warehouse; they're apartments. Fifty-four rental units, no two the same, each more irresistible than the next. The oak columns still bear nineteenth-century stenciling in black on whitewash: NO COTTON BALES HIGHER THAN HERE. Oak ceiling beams display stenciled numbers, a means of warehouse reference. Custommade doors accommodate the old, high doorways, and the bathrooms are cavernous. There's a three-story glassed-in atrium. Everywhere, there is original wood—wide-plank floors, chamfered columns, pillars from old-growth pine trees that must have been seventy-five feet tall, and a ceiling of wood, too, so vast and high I couldn't tell you whether it's pine or oak. On the sprawling roof deck, you feel as though you're on the roof of New York, because the tip of Manhattan and the Lower East Side are spread out in front of you. You can also see New York Harbor, Ellis Island, the Statue of Liberty, Governors Island, the Verrazano-Narrows Bridge, Staten Island, and the Goethals Bridge. The *Queen Mary* cruises in, steams past, and docks right around the corner from us on Easter Sunday.

The second floor of the building houses Fairway's kitchens and some office spaces and activity areas given to community groups. The ground floor is the market—and it's huge.

Glazed Carrot Puree with Fresh Ginger

Serves 4

The final step in this recipe makes the result sublime: you reduce the cooking water to a rich glaze, then use it to sweeten and enrich the carrot puree.

1 bunch carrots (about 5 medium), scrubbed and cut into ¼-inch rounds

1 tablespoon unsalted butter

1 to 2 teaspoons grated fresh ginger

Kosher or sea salt and freshly ground black pepper

1. Place the carrots in a medium saucepan with water to cover. Add the butter and bring to a boil. Simmer until the carrots are tender, about 5 minutes.

2. Use a slotted spoon to transfer the carrots to a food processor or blender, leaving the cooking liquid in the saucepan. Add the ginger and puree until smooth. Season with salt and pepper to taste.

3. Return the carrot cooking water to a simmer, then reduce the heat to medium-low and simmer, taking care not to burn the liquid (there are a lot of natural sugars from the carrots in it), until the liquid is reduced to about 2 tablespoons and is syrupy, about 15 minutes. Add this glaze to the puree and pulse to blend. Serve immediately or rewarm before serving.

Chef's Note: People love this, I think because it's a great, brilliant color and everybody loves ginger.

Weird weather. Yeah, a lot of rain, but more than that—weird. Feels weird. Not bad weird—pretty good, actually. Not too hot, not too muggy, though today certainly is. Nice breeze. But at night, it feels spooky. Ghosts and stuff. Night wind whipping up the glorious elms and bushes of the park. Low-hanging scud and strati clouds racing, racing north across the night sky. Saw my first lightning bugs of the season a couple of nights ago. You probably call them fireflies. Where I'm from it's lightning bugs. Smells so good, at least up here in Morningside Heights, Riverside Park. It's the linden trees. Right now the lindens' blowsy boughs are pendulous with blossoms. So fragrant. Picked some off a tree Sunday on Randalls Island where the boys and I play tennis (and have played religiously for years).

English and French people revere lindens for their blossoms. They dry these blossoms and make a hot beverage out of them. The French call it an infusion. The flavor is very pleasant, and the infusion is restorative and calming; it used to be considered a panacea. *Tilleul* (pronounced "tee-YUL") is French for linden. For some reason, the English translation of *tilleul* is "lime tree," so that to this day, many people think they're drinking an infusion made with lime tree blossoms, a citrus flower. No. Those lime trees are not linden trees.

We import *tilleul* from a Frenchwoman who works a farm just south of Paris, near Versailles. Her specialty, though, is peppermint, which she also packs in cellophane "sachets" as an infusion. And verbena and hibiscus, which make marvelous iced tea. I just got in a quantity of each, and I'm going to have them out in Red Hook hanging on vertical clip hangers in the coffee and tea area.

A funny thing happened the day before we opened the Red Hook store. At least it seems funny now—it didn't at the time. Around noon on the day before the idiotic grand opening, we're all a bunch of frantic zombies racing about, and suddenly the power goes out. *Tink.* Black. Lights, refrigeration, scales, computers, cash registers, everything.

At this point our highly vaunted, Al Gore–commemorative, revolutionary, ecofriendly, never-done-before, private on-the-premises power plant is designed to kick in, thereby obviating the need to involve Con Edison. In fact, the only reason we were on the Con Ed grid at that moment was that some timing process was being actuated at our power plant (all right—I don't know what "actuated" is supposed to mean, but that's the information they gave us). Nevertheless, our power plant, a separate, unassuming brick structure on the west side of the parking lot, proceeded to lie there like lox, delivering zero power.

All hands milled about the parking lot for four bloody hours, while our aspiring technical geniuses dithered and massaged and tweaked and shrugged. Howie—who was actually and unbelievably very cool during the whole episode, rather than treating us to his usual Yosemite Sam routine—finally found himself poised to throw the master switch inside the power plant, putting an end to the outage. He tells me he almost wished that when he did throw the switch, the whole building, historically significant pre–Civil War structure or not, would blow up as if it had been hit by a tactical nuclear weapon. That Howie. What a card.

It didn't blow up. The power came on, everything refrigerated was still cold; everything frozen was still frozen; etc. All it meant was that we could tack on four more hours to the prodigious mountain of work we still had to do. Great. Just what we needed.

That didn't turn out to be a bad omen, though. We hired scores of locals to work at the Red Hook store, and they are among the sweetest, most earnest people I have ever encountered. All our longtimers who came over to the Brooklyn store have been superb, of course. Bricks. I couldn't be prouder of our employees.

And the shoppers, our customers—doubtless thirty-nine out of forty are Brooklynites—are the nicest I could ever have imagined: the most supportive, the most food-savvy, and genuinely excited about the store. At first they were so appreciative and inquisitive about food and cooking that I kept thinking they were putting me on. It was like being out of state. I guess we got the feng shui right with the place, but I don't know.

At this writing, Fairway is a four-store business. Doubtless there will be other stores, *tout de suite. À fond de train!* (Full speed ahead!)

Curried Cauliflower Bisque with Parmesan-Garlic Crostini

Serves 8

This is very delicious, very satisfying, and very easy, and there's *no* cream. It used to be very cheap, too, until cauliflower got fashionable.

4 to 6 tablespoons unsalted butter

1 medium Spanish onion, peeled and thinly sliced (about 3 cups)

1 small leek, well cleaned (see Chef's Note, page 217), white part only, chopped

1 tablespoon kosher salt, plus additional to taste

2 large heads cauliflower, cut into medium-size florets

1 large russet potato, peeled and roughly chopped

1 teaspoon curry powder, plus additional to taste

2 quarts all-purpose chicken stock, preferably homemade (see recipe, page 116)

½ teaspoon ground white pepper, plus additional to taste

¼ cup grated Parmesan cheese (optional)

2 tablespoons finely chopped chives

8 Parmesan-Garlic Crostini (recipe follows), optional

1. In a large, heavy stockpot over medium-low heat, melt 4 tablespoons of the butter. Add the onion and leek and a pinch of salt and cook over low heat until the vegetables are softened and translucent, about 20 minutes. Stir often and adjust the heat if necessary so that the vegetables do not brown.

2. Add the cauliflower, potato, and curry powder and cook, stirring often, until the cauliflower and potato have begun to soften, about 20 minutes. (If the contents of the pot start to brown, lower the heat or slide the pot off the center of the flame and stir like mad!)

3. Add the chicken stock, raise the heat to high, and bring the soup to a boil. Reduce the heat and keep the soup at a gentle simmer until the cauliflower is totally soft, about 30 more minutes.

4. Working carefully, puree the soup in batches in a food processor, or use an immersion blender. Season with salt and white pepper, and, if desired, more curry powder. Optional: In order to achieve a supersmooth, bisquelike texture, I like to pass the soup through a fine sieve.

5. When you are ready to serve the soup, return it to the pot and bring it back to a simmer. Stir in the remaining 2 tablespoons of cold butter, if desired, and the Parmesan cheese. Test again for seasonings and dish it up hot, hot, hot. Add a sprinkle of chopped chives to each soup bowl and serve with Parmesan-Garlic Crostini.

Parmesan-Garlic Crostini with Crouton Variation

Makes 15 to 20 large crostini, or 4 cups croutons

These are a great accompaniment to hearty soups and—if cut smaller—are "up the ante" croutons for Caesar salad (see page 175).

1. Preheat the oven to 350°F.
2. For large crostini, slice the baguette on the bias into thick, even slices (this will give you maximum surface area for your garlic and Parmesan). Lay the slices on a sheet pan and brush the top sides with olive oil. Toast in the oven until lightly golden, 5 to 7 minutes. Rub the top of each piece of toast with a garlic clove. Sprinkle the crostini with the grated cheese and return them to the oven until the cheese melts, about 2 minutes more.
3. For croutons, smash 1 peeled garlic clove and place it in a large bowl. Add the olive oil and let the mixture infuse for 20 minutes, then remove the garlic. Slice the baguette into thick, even slices, then cut the slices into large (about ¾-inch) cubes. Toss the cubes in the garlic-infused olive oil until well coated but not saturated. Use a slotted spoon to transfer the cubes to a rimmed baking sheet and spread them in a single layer. Toast, tossing halfway through the cooking time, until light golden, 5 to 7 minutes. Sprinkle with the grated cheese and return the pan to the oven until the cheese melts, about 2 minutes more.

1 large sourdough baguette
¼ cup extra-virgin olive oil
1 to 2 large garlic cloves, peeled
½ cup coarsely grated Parmesan cheese

Chef's Note: When you're making the large crostini, there is no need to cut the garlic cloves before rubbing the bread with them. The bread's surface is abrasive enough to extract the juices. Just make sure all the peel is removed.

7

How to Shop
Like a
Fairway Regular

We New Yorkers shop for food every day. New York is not like much of the rest of the country, where people visit a grocery store once a week. Apartment pantries, for most of us, are small, if we have a pantry at all. Most refrigerators are small, too, and forget about separate deep freezers. Out in the heartland, I seem to remember, every household had a deep freezer, a big old lift-top coffinlike monstrosity. God knows what people put in it. Catfish, bass, bluegill? Venison? Body parts? Frozen food never occurs to many of us New Yorkers. We live from fresh meal to fresh meal. This is probably why those of us who work at Fairway are so familiar with so many of our customers; we see them almost every day. We are invested in each other.

I can't tell you how many people consider me a personal friend—and I consider them special friends of mine too. Often I couldn't tell you their names if my life depended on it, even when I've "known" them for years. But should I run into them in some other part of the city, as happens all the time, or in some other state, or even in Europe—and believe me, that happens frequently—we are overjoyed to see each other. These people consider me and the others at Fairway to be their personal grocers.

"Steven, what are we having for dinner tonight?"

"Well, what did you have last night?"

"Ah, we went out. Some dumb restaurant."

"You can say that again. Shame on you. You know, I just passed by Danny and his seafood, and I saw some wild sea scallops that looked heavenly. I'm going to take two of them—they're huge—for each of us in my family, and a couple of those giant prawns, too, for each of us. I'm going to peel the prawns and roll them and the scallops in bread crumbs with a lot of salt and pepper and some hot red chile flakes. I'm going to use the bread crumbs we grind from our own bread, rather than those industrial ones in the can. And I'm not going to use *panko* (Japanese bread crumbs), because for some reason they get on my wife's nerves. A lot of salt and pepper. Then I'll sauté them in a pan with olive oil and garlic and maybe some fresh minced savory and thyme at the very end. I'll serve the scallops and prawns with some fat sugar snaps that I've turned around in a pan with those tiny white potatoes. I'll steam the spuds first for a few minutes. And I'll use butter instead of olive oil. Fast, easy, very satisfying. Nothing to it."

The truth is that both our kids are away, and Michelle and I are going over to Margo and Robert's place to share takeout barbecue—and who's to know what a lousy cook I am, anyway? Michelle's the cook.

But the point here is this: just try to have an experience like this in a supermarket someplace. It probably isn't going to happen. First of all, there's rarely anyone on the floor of a supermarket to engage in the first place, much less someone who recognizes you, who knows you. And if there were such

How to Shop: Three Rules

1. Find a store that knows food, knows you, and knows what you're having for dinner tonight.
2. Don't go shopping hungry, if you don't want to end up at your apartment with a lot of stuff you can't even remember putting in the shopping cart. At Fairway, we've got so much wonderful stuff you'd never, ever find in another store that if you come hungry, you might as well just let one of us lift you up, turn you upside down, and shake you until all the cash and credit cards fall out of your pockets. Forget about lingering at my cheese counter. It'll cost you.
3. Be invisible. Convince yourself you're invisible. Pay not a whit of attention to how crowded it is. Make believe you're the only shopper in the place. This serves two purposes: first, you won't feel that you have to hurry; and second, you'll be able to give the food your complete attention.

people, and if they did recognize you—these supermarket employees whose passion for food is on a par with their passion for philately—I doubt seriously that they could conjure up a vision of a meal that would be memorable for any of us.

So in this regard, Fairway looms large in the lives of many people, and will continue to do so for as long as they shop with us. We are invested in their lives—in their food lives—and we care as much about their pleasure as we do about ours.

Though I can't prove it, I have reason to believe that the original Fairway Market does more business (in dollars) per square foot than any other food store in the world. Several people in a position to know arcane stuff such as this—retail consultants, supermarket industry reporters, bankers, and Wall Street guys—have sworn that it's a fact. This means that the store is almost always crowded, except for very early in the morning and very late at night—or when it's pouring or there's a blizzard.

FAIRWAY
"Like No Other Market"

OUR GARBER FAMILY
LOUISIANA
★YAMS★

ARE EXTRAORDINARY–
A MEAL IN THEMSELVES.

STAB THEM WITH A FORK, RUB (COAT) LIBERALLY
WITH FAIRWAY EXTRA VIRGIN OLIVE OIL, SALT
AND PEPPER, DO NOT WRAP THEM
IN FOIL, PLACE IN BAKING PAN, BAKE
ONE HOUR AT 425, SERVE WITH IMPORTED
GREEK TOTAL BRAND WHOLE MILK YOGURT.

The bright blue awning of the store sweeps impressively from 74th Street almost all the way to 75th. Beneath it is a vibrant, tantalizing array of vegetables and fruit. The sidewalk is almost always a seething river of people headed in both directions, many of whom have made a beeline for this very destination. The problem is that most people are irritable before they've even picked something up from the outside bins. Broadway at 74th Street is a very busy intersection and sidewalk.

At any given time, in addition to the double-parked fire engines and trucks on the street, the sidewalk is usually clogged with an assortment of nitwits pursuing their tiresome agendas. People set up card tables right outside in an ongoing attempt to register voters. Here in New York, it seems there's always an imminent election, so politicians running for whatever office use the sidewalk in front of Fairway as their personal soapbox and their place to meet and greet.

Taxi drivers pull up as close to the store as they can and idle while waiting for customers laden with shopping bags to fall out of the store and into their cabs.

There are the guys who hawk cheap jewelry, peacock feathers, and socks. Once one of them was selling tiny violins complete with bow and a felt-lined violin case. And there's the damnable horn man, an old fellow with a battered silver trumpet. His extremely limited repertoire includes the theme from *The Pink Panther,* the theme from *The Godfather,* the theme from *Cabaret,* "Go Tell Aunt Rhody," "Go Tell It on the Mountain," "Over the Rainbow," "Knick Knack Paddywhack," "New York, New York," and "My Way." As if these tunes weren't the equivalent of a fingernail being scraped across a blackboard,

the guy has a bad case of hornblower's apnea. To make that even worse, his tempo for every song is so sclerotic that should you find yourself attempting to sing or whistle along, you find yourself eternally three or four bars ahead of him. And suddenly the horn apnea kicks in. He stops blowing in mid-bar for a few beats, then rouses himself, and starts back up right where he left off before he stopped breathing. But he and I recently came to an agreement; we have an understanding. I go out on the street and drop a five-dollar bill in his trumpet case and he goes away for the rest of the day.

In short, it's a crush of humanity. Just getting past the front door into the store is an exercise in road rage, one-upmanship, and type-A aggressiveness. As you pass the threshold, you are blasted by the blower—hot air in cold months and cold air in hot months. It is as if you were being sanitized, as if we were trying to blow the irritation off you so that you can be a more pliant and amenable shopper.

You made it; you're inside. Welcome to the sanctum sanctorum. Fairway. Like no other market.

As regards your perambulation about the store, don't be passive. If you're pushing a cart, be decisive. Shoot right around dawdlers. But you needn't be reckless or thoughtless. Don't feel that you can't turn around and go back for another pass at the fruits and vegetables. This is where convincing yourself that you're invisible comes into play. What do you care if somebody gives you a dirty look? This is *your* store, and you must feel empowered to shop here *your* way. But do try not to smash your shopping cart into someone's Achilles tendon. It happens all the time. Regular Fairway shoppers are easy to pick out of a crowd. They're the ones with the permanent limp. It's so embarrassing to bash someone else's Achilles tendon. There's just nothing you can say to make him or her stop hurting. It's a toss-up as to whether I'd rather take a bash or give one. Both accidents are unpleasant, but they're also both real statistics, and there's just nothing that can be done. They are simply a part of life.

Immediately on reaching a service counter, take a number. If there are no numbers, or if the machine is empty, just intone to no one in particular, "Are you taking numbers today?" In this manner, you will not find yourself standing there like a fool, pointlessly, for what seems like an eternity. If we

Seafood counter at the Upper West Side store.

Asparagus with Parmesan

Freshly shaved Parmesan is essential to this dish, as is freshly ground black pepper. There is no better way to eat asparagus.

1¼ pounds medium green asparagus, woody ends broken off, remaining bottom 3 inches peeled

Fresh juice of ½ lemon

1 tablespoon unsalted butter, cut into small pieces

Kosher or sea salt and freshly ground black pepper

3 tablespoons freshly grated Parmesan cheese

1. Preheat the broiler for 15 to 20 minutes.
2. Arrange the asparagus in a single layer in a large, very shallow oven-proof skillet. Add water to cover the asparagus halfway and bring the water to a boil. Simmer for 2 minutes.
3. Drain the asparagus and return it to the skillet. Squeeze lemon juice over all, dot with butter, season with salt and pepper, and sprinkle with the Parmesan. Broil, watching closely until the Parmesan is completely melted and beginning to brown, 2 to 3 minutes. Serve immediately.

Grocer's Note: We always think of asparagus as a springtime vegetable, but this is just not so anymore. Asparagus is grand all year now. Just choose spears that have dark, tight, unbroken tips and no wrinkles on the shafts. Don't equivocate over whether the best asparagus is skinny or fat. That makes no difference whatsoever, no matter what you've been told. Really, the only advantage to skinny asparagus is that often, it needn't be peeled. Store "grass" (that's an industry term) in a plastic bag in the vegetable hamper and use it up that day or within a few days. Freshness is paramount to asparagus.

aren't taking numbers, at least your presence and desire to be waited on will be registered. Don't let people jump in front of you. Zealously guard the place you have earned on line. Well, it's not a line you'll be waiting on (or "in," as the rest of the country says). It's not even a queue. It's a crowd, a gaggle, a throng. Very different, dynamically, from a line. Note who was there before you and who came after you. If you allow even one person who got there after you to greet a counterman and ask for a quarter-pound of kosher salami sliced not too thin and not too thick, you're finished.

When your turn finally comes, speak up proudly and say that indeed you are number ninety-eight, and approach the counter. Look the counterman right in the eye, smile, and say hello to him. At Fairway—unlike the famous Katz's Deli downtown on Houston Street ("Send a salami to your boy in the army!")—you do not tip the counterman. Tips are a veritable 401K for the guys at Katz's. There, when you tip the counterman, you get a taste of the pastrami or the corned beef. At Fairway you can taste anything you want without the baksheesh—no problem. So, no tip. But it certainly helps to be nice.

Niceness rules at Fairway, and everywhere else, at least in my experience. Everybody should just be nice, and the world would be a lovely place. People respond to niceness. It's a wonder so few people understand that. And being nice has a compound effect. Let's say you've been (or "made") nice with the same counterman at prepared foods and deli and appy about fourteen times over the last month or two. That counterman is going to look out for you in ways you can take to the bank. *Lots* of tastes. Frequent extra slices at no charge. The best-looking portions of stuffed cabbage. The rarest roast beef. Quarts of beef stew with all ingredients well represented, and plenty of gravy. Lids clamped on tight. Saran overwraps, just in case something is leaky. Patience with you as he hands you packages over the Lucite sneeze guard, rather than a tight-lipped grimace as you juggle and drop. A knish or a spear of asparagus for your child who is sitting in the shopping cart.

Children. If your child is miserable here, you're going to be miserable. If your kid is cranky and you're on your way to Fairway or on your way home via

Fairway, it is advisable to consider dropping the kid at the apartment, tying the little sweetie securely to something, and then going out to shop. Whinging, whining, crying children in Fairway are a constant. If your child is acting up, prepare to be publicly humiliated. And if you have the gall to come in here with a double-wide stroller, you can bet you're going to be publicly humiliated. If you can take it, OK; come right ahead with the double-wide.

You know, that's the whole thing. Those supermarkets out there in the hinterland have aisles wider than most New Yorkers' living rooms. And tell your kids not to touch anything. If I see one of your children pick up a twenty-dollar bottle of balsamic vinegar just for the hell of it, I'm going to snatch it away from him (her, whatever), glare at you, and hope you get indignant.

Firemen and Fairway

If I were asked to articulate my own personal mental image of Fairway Market at 74th Street and Broadway, after having worked there since 1980, what would float before my closed eyes would be, in no particular order, old ladies, pretty girls, cops, and firemen. There always seems to be a fire engine idling outside, and a squad car or two. Firemen and cops love Fairway. Of this there is no doubt. Those of us who prowl the floor at Fairway know a lot of these uniformed guys and gals personally. They're regulars, just like you. So the events of September 11, 2001, hit us pretty hard, because we lost a lot of them—folks who, if they failed to show up for a few days, would be missed. We'd wonder where they were.

As you might imagine, we were immediately descended on by the Red Cross, various city agencies, and the Salvation Army, imploring us to supply all sorts of relief material for downtown. Of course, we did. Mountains of stuff. Not just coffee, water, juice, fruit, and sandwiches, but stuff that shouted out what was really going on down there. Eyedrops, mouthwash, rubbing alcohol, bleach, throat lozenges, batteries, PowerBars, even rubber gloves. What the relief workers didn't know—certainly our customers didn't know it—was that Fairway was already spearheading the collection, transfer, and delivery of tons of food directly to the disaster site, or at least to the Chelsea Piers, where the food was loaded onto ferries that scooted right down to Ground Zero, where our trucks couldn't go. And we told no one about our efforts. All we cared about was showing up and being there to take whatever measure of responsibility we could. To do something, for God's sake. Not just stand there. Our cops and firemen sure as hell didn't just stand there. Our regulars. Bless their hearts.

After all, shopping here is not a right; it's a privilege. You have to know how to conduct yourself.

I once watched the legendary David Sneddon have an encounter with a woman who was complaining about something. After he had applied all the patience he could muster; after he had explained to her that sometimes a truck is late, or that sometimes we do run out of things, or that of course her cheese is moldy—you bought it two months ago and now you want your money back?—or something equally infuriating, I heard him tell her that perhaps she wasn't mature enough to shop at Fairway. Very Gandhi of him.

ere's another reason there isn't tons of space in the Fairway aisles: restocking. Ninety-nine percent of the humdrum supermarkets in the United States do so little business that restocking is not an issue. In fact, most of them have a night crew that gets the restocking done in a few hours, with the stuff coming off one or maybe two not-so-big trucks. Here at Fairway, restocking is an all-day and all-night affair.

Oy, the honking on Broadway. At holiday times—Jewish holidays, Thanksgiving, and Christmas—truckers have to make appointments with our receiving guys just to get a slot to make a drop. Some of them show up at three or four AM to get

in line for a late-morning delivery. So we're constantly restocking, lest the shelves be emptied. Fairway is the very definition of critical mass: there is only so much stuff we can receive and send to the basement, and only so much stuff we can bring up from the basement, stock on the shelves, and pack into grocery shopping bags.

There are three pieces of rolling equipment that enable us to restock the shelves. One is a hand truck. Where I come from, this is called a dolly, so in 1973, when I was driving a truck and making deliveries of jugs and bottles of Mountain Valley Spring Water from Hot Springs, Arkansas, before water became a fad, even before Perrier, the first time at the warehouse, in front of my fellow drivers, Irish Teamsters all, I referred to my hand truck as a dolly. They took some cord, tied me faceup to an empty pallet, hoisted the pallet as high as the forklift would go, and left.

We don't use dollies—I mean hand trucks—much, because they hold only about five or six cases of anything, and that's not very efficient. Occasionally, Juan Pablo Tolentino and his men use them to get a few incredibly heavy cases of fluid dairy products up from the basement. Juan Pablo is the best dairyman in the history of supermarket dairymen, and that's impressive, because the supermarket dairyman has one of the worst jobs in the store. Everything he deals with is heavy, wet, cold, sometimes sticky, sometimes smelly, and so perishable that it spoils if you look at it funny. Everything has to be squared away at four AM every day. Miles of dairy shelves and the basement dairy walk-in refrigerators end up slick with milk, cream, sour cream, and whatever else, and have to be scrubbed down. There's box after box, filled with carton after carton of broken or out-of-date eggs. Did you ever smell dank broken eggs that have been lying around a cold refrigerator?

Juan Pablo is a Zen master. Imagine a thirty-year career of that stuff in tandem with watching old ladies and old gentlemen open up four-stick boxes of butter to extract the single stick they want. Then they remove the lid from the cottage cheese container, break the seal, give the cottage cheese a sniff, replace the lid, put the container back in the wrong place, and shuffle off. They've decided they didn't really need any, and besides, it didn't smell fresh. They open a carton of eggs, lift and inspect each egg for cracks, and drop one of them—then close the carton and shuffle off. Didn't really need eggs, either.

Second, we use the hollywood. That's a sturdy steel cart with a handle on one end to guide it. As to why it is called a hollywood, well, there you have me. I can't get a plausible answer from anybody in the business, and that includes the people who make the carts. Hollywoods are omnipresent, and they're Fairway-friendly.

Finally, there's the U-boat, the main form of transportation for Fairway's goods. It's five feet long and about eighteen inches wide, a flat cart about six inches off the ground, on six little wheels arranged two by two. The bed is made of wood framed by steel; the rest of the contraption is steel, too—posts rise from each corner of the flat bed and join at each end to create a U shape.

OPPOSITE PAGE:
Checking out at the Upper West Side store.

All-Purpose Chicken Stock and Creamy Chicken Soup with Orzo Variation

Mitchel's big on chicken soup. It's a Jewish thing, maybe. In addition to being useful whenever a full-flavored chicken broth is called for, this stock absolutely makes the cream-free yet creamy chicken soup that follows. It is supremely satisfying, a true comfort food that'll smooth even the most frazzled nerves and cure the common cold. But don't try any shortcuts. If you can't make the stock, don't make the soup!

All-Purpose Chicken Stock

Makes about 2½ quarts

6 pounds chicken necks and backs

3 large carrots, unpeeled, scrubbed and roughly chopped

½ bunch of celery with tops, roughly chopped

1 large Spanish onion, roughly chopped (no need to peel)

Stems from ½ bunch flat-leaf parsley, roughly chopped (the leaves won't harm the stock but you can save them for another use)

1 sprig fresh thyme

8 whole peppercorns

1. Preheat the oven to 450°F. Spread the chicken necks and backs on two rimmed baking sheets and roast, reversing the pans from front to back and top to bottom, halfway through the cooking time, until the chicken is golden brown, about 45 minutes. Transfer the chicken to a large stockpot, leaving the fat behind.

2. Add the remaining ingredients to the stockpot, along with enough water to just cover (about 1 gallon). Bring to a boil, then lower to a simmer. Simmer gently, skimming the fat and foam from the surface frequently, for at least 4 hours and up to 5 hours (longer cooking yields a more concentrated broth). Strain and let cool.

Creamy Chicken Soup with Orzo Variation

Serves 6

1. Bring the chicken stock to a boil and season to taste with salt and pepper.

2. Meanwhile, make a roux by melting the butter in a pan over low heat. Gradually stir in the flour and cook, stirring often, until the roux is golden-brown, about 30 minutes. Let cool completely.

3. Place 2 tablespoons of the cooled roux in a large glass measuring cup and gradually whisk in a ladleful of the hot stock until smoothly combined. Whisk this mixture back into the simmering stock and continue to simmer for 30 minutes. Taste the soup and whisk in a little more of the roux if a creamier soup is desired.

4. Cook the orzo in boiling salted water until just tender, about 7 minutes. Add to the soup and serve.

2½ quarts All-Purpose Chicken Stock (see Chef's Note)

Kosher or sea salt and freshly ground white pepper, to taste

4 tablespoons unsalted butter

⅓ cup flour

¼ pound (¾ cup) orzo

Chef's Note: I feel very strongly that this soup needs to be made from scratch. Since it is all about *chicken flavor,* it's important that the base be made from *chicken,* so please begin by making the All-Purpose Chicken Stock.

Grocer's Note: Orzo is a Greek pasta, a staple used mostly in salads. The name means "rice," because the shape of the pasta resembles that of a grain of rice.

8

The Dark Ages of Cheese in New York, and

How the Enlightenment Dawned

I want to go back to 1980 for a minute. What was the serious cheese scene in New York at that time?

There was no cheese. Oh, there was cheese. But I mean there was no cheese made by people, rather than machinery. Serious cheese is made from raw (unpasteurized) milk. Ninety-nine percent of all serious cheeses have been made by the same families, using the same old-fashioned tools and recipes and methods, for centuries. Many of the names of these cheeses are well-known, at least by Europeans. Most of the names come from the village nearest to the farm or to the facility where the cheese is made. When I came to Fairway, serious cheese was 99.99 percent European (with 0.01 percent Oka from Quebec, Grafton Cheddar and Crowley Cheese from Vermont, a few farmstead Wisconsin cheeses, and California Vella Dry

Jack and Teleme). The few French and Italian cheeses being imported in those days were factory cheeses, imitations of the originals. Spanish cheeses, including the now ubiquitous Manchego, were unheard of. English exported cheeses were a joke. Cheddar, Cheshire, Caerphilly, and Gloucester were phony factory imitations, differing from each other only in color. Sage Derby, a vile concoction, looked and tasted like Irish Spring soap. And New Yorkers actually thought Blarney was a worthwhile Irish cheese.

I suppose the worst of the lot were the Scandinavian cheeses. At that time, the easiest and most profitable way to make money importing cheese was to get the cheap, nourishing factory cheeses of Denmark, Norway, Sweden, and Finland. Finlandia Swiss aside, the Scandinavian cheeses could be described as flabby, glossy, and bland. Swiss cheeses were there, and Swiss cheeses are grand—also sturdy and therefore easy to import. But despite my respect for them, they are pretty much one-note Johnnies.

The cheese we had access to from Italy was laughable. Grana Padano, a

Shaved Fennel and Parmesan Salad

Serves 4

This is a good side salad with a fresh, summery flavor. For this recipe, I like a complex, robust olive oil, such as an unfiltered Barbera Sicilian, an Andalusian Baena, an Extremaduran Gata-Hurdes, or a Tuscan or Umbrian. And be sure to use real Parmigiano-Reggiano—no other "Parmesan" will do.

1. Slice the fennel very thinly (either by hand, with a mandoline, or with the shaving side of a box grater).
2. Using a cheese plane (or the shaving side of a box grater), thinly shave the cheese.
3. In a salad bowl, toss the fennel with the olive oil, lemon juice, and salt. Season with pepper to taste, and top with the shaved Parmigiano and parsley.

2 medium fennel bulbs, trimmed

8 ounces Parmigiano-Reggiano

¼ cup extra-virgin olive oil

2 tablespoons fresh lemon juice

1 teaspoon kosher or sea salt

Freshly ground black pepper, to taste

¼ cup coarsely chopped flat-leaf parsley

Chef's Note: Fennel bulbs, also called anise, are underappreciated. They can be cut into endless interesting shapes—dice, slivers, matchsticks, shavings, medallions—and then served raw, steamed, sautéed, roasted, etc. Most people who are skeptical about fennel just haven't found a recipe that's right for it.

This summer the best tomatoes have been those Campari tomatoes in the rectangular clear plastic containers; and they don't really qualify as summer stuff, because they're so agribusiness—nothing grower-holy or local about them. They're trucked here from Mexico. But, damn, they're good with one of those *burrata* cheeses we fly in every week from Campania, the region of Naples, from the hills behind Salerno. *Burrata* is a rarefied *fior di latte*, a name which means "flower of milk" and is correct for Italian-origin mozzarella made from cow's milk. Mozzarella is made from the milk of the water buffalo (*bufala*). Let the Italians differentiate. I say *burrata* is rarefied because it is wrapped-around shreds of *fior di latte*, plus thick sweet cream, plus whey to form this wondrous, otherwise amorphous cheese that looks like a gland. Then that is wrapped in asphodel leaves, which are (logically) indigenous, and the leaves perfume the cheese with an indescribable fragrance. You simply plop it onto a plate, lop the thing into bite-size pieces, add the quartered Campari tomatoes, pepper the heck out of the whole thing, and drizzle one of my marvelous barrel oils over it. I guarantee you you'll feel that this is the best summer of your life, whether you've been swimming or not.

very respectable grating cheese (*grana* = grain, that is, a cheese which when grated yields grains), was omnipresent; but as for Parmigiano-Reggiano, well, its availability was spotty at best. In those days, there was no perception that the only Parmesan is Parmigiano-Reggiano, much less that Parmigiano-Reggiano is the world's greatest cheese. Romano was easy to find, but I confess that it's never found in our kitchen at home. I just don't have the right gene. It smells like throw-up to me. I'm being irrational, I dutifully admit—this is a confession, after all.

No Fontina d'Aosta, one of the world's five greatest cheeses. I brought it to New York in 1979, so Fontina, the ultimate melter, actually had just shown up then. What a coup that was! The Taleggio and stracchino here were a joke. Factory-made outrages from the biggest dairy concern in northern Italy. I fixed that. No Pecorino Toscano. I fixed that times about twelve; I was and still am a lover of the sheep's milk cheeses of Tuscany, Umbria, Le Marche, and Sardinia (not to mention Portugal and both sides of the Pyrenees—hang on, we'll get there). Absolutely zero cheeses from Piedmont, the amazingly prolific food and wine region of northeastern Italy. These are cheeses so numerous and visually variable (in size, shape, and color) that my displays of them, once I got them, made the cheese counter look like a fireworks stand.

In the winter of 1980, New York cheese shops had no *mozzarella di bufala,* no *burrata* (a latecomer even for me—it began to be flown in only a couple of years ago), no aged Gorgonzola. No real Asiago from the northern Veneto—only a hard, sharp impostor from the Stella factories in Wisconsin and Ohio. No Montasio from Friuli (except at Todaro Brothers in Manhattan's Turtle Bay, a neighborhood with many Sicilians and Armenians who would purchase Montasio by the quarter wheel). There was nothing, really, unless you had the good fortune to live near or travel frequently to an Italian shop in Little Italy, Brooklyn, or Staten Island where Sicilian *ricotta salata* and *pepato* and Calabrian incanestrato and Crotonese were staples, as were caciocavallo from Puglia and provolone from Campania. But these southern Italian cheeses were never a passion of mine. They just were. As was fresh mozzarella.

New York has always been a treasure trove for fresh mozzarella, hand-pulled (in small batches) several times daily, delivered warm and never refrigerated—refrigeration quickly ruins the texture and flavor. No self-respecting cheese shop or cheese department could be without fresh mozzarella, no

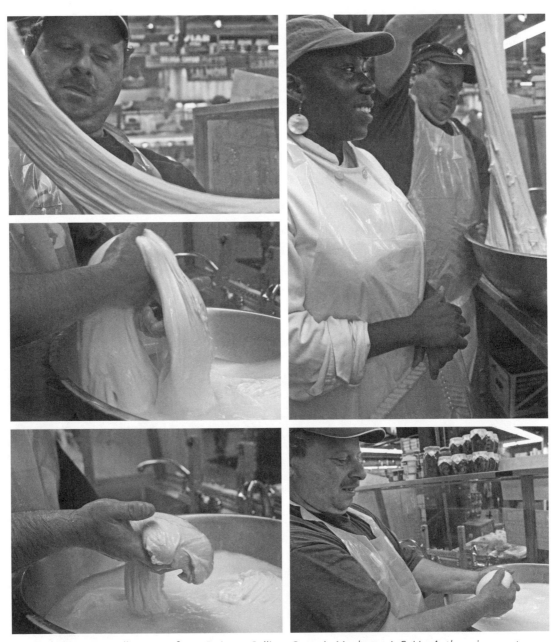

Anthony Campanelli, owner of Joe's Dairy on Sullivan Street in Manhattan's SoHo; Anthony is a master cheesemaker, among the finest people I have ever met, and his mother threw out the letter sent to him by the New York Mets inviting him to spring training (back in, oh, 1973 or so), Anthony having mightily impressed them as a walk-on tryout. She was afraid he would turn his back on the family store. Anthony has taught us how to make the city's best mozzarella.

matter how Frenchified it wanted to be. These days each of our stores makes mozzarella on the premises.

By the time I fell into Fairway, I had realized—thank you, sweet Jesus—that New Yorkers had never tasted real Brie or real Camembert, reblochon, Epoisses, Munster d'Alsace, Livarot, and Pont-l'Evêque. All those *fromages de chèvre* with the lilting, lyrical names of nearby villages: the Auvergnat cheeses, gaperon, Fourme d'Ambert, Bleu des Causses, Cantal, Salers, Laguiole, and others. Arguably, the Auvergne region, often referred to as the Massif Central, in the middle of France, is the most prolific great cheese-producing region in the world. And none of its cheeses were here in New York.

There were no Spanish or Portuguese cheeses. Nor were there even a few American cheeses of any remark, but in those days the American cheese-making revolution was just beginning.

I ought to say that I have never had an original thought in my life—certainly not about how these cheeses and other goods at Fairway should be displayed and sold, once I figured out how to get them. I've stolen every idea that made me successful. Everything I'm talking about now I picked up hanging out—for hours—at street markets in Paris and other cities in Europe, at famous French cheese shops, at the shops of fishmongers and butchers. I would arrive before dawn to watch them set up, and I would linger until long after dusk watching the shopkeepers and stand operators pack up and put their businesses to bed. That's how I learned what makes cheese shops great, what they carry, how they handle it, how they make it look.

Foremost, a great cheese shop must offer the fresh stuff. Farm eggs and fresh cream. Crème fraîche and block butter. Gumless cream cheese and ricotta from small dairies. There's a world of difference between Polly-O and small dairy ricotta, not to mention the difference between cow's milk ricotta and *real* ricotta, which is made from the whey of sheep's milk, a by-product of the production of Pecorino Romano.

To understand the value of serious ricotta, as opposed to that stuff you find in the dairy section of most supermarkets, try this experiment at mealtime. Sauté handfuls of fresh spinach in olive oil with coarsely chopped onion and minced or whole cloves of garlic. Toss the spinach with rotelle (wagon wheels), conchiglie (shells), or fusilli (spirals) and fresh sheep's milk ricotta and then blanket it with grated Parmigiano. Michelle and I took this recipe from Marcella Hazan.

You'll see what I'm saying.

So I taught myself about gastronomy by going to all the places where famous foods, and specifically cheeses, came from. I read every food book I could get my hands on. I knew what wasn't available to my customers. I made it my business to provide those things for them, and that meant I had to import.

Starting with France—Normandy. Pont-l'Evêque, Livarot, *real* Camembert, Pavé d'Auges, crème fraîche, and butter. *Real* Brie from Brie, a cheese in its original state as different from the loathsome factory-made version as Spam is from foie gras. Well, every one of those earthshaking cheeses was then and is now, unless it's made from pasteurized milk, illegal.

Thanks to travel and study, my knowledge of cheeses had gotten way beyond what I was able to sell at Fairway. I had no *real* cheeses. I had no— well, the list was endless, as I've made clear. How could I call myself a master cheesemonger? It was like being a librarian whose shelves had no Mark Twain, William Faulkner, or Ernest Hemingway. So what I did was place "whistling in the dark" orders for these cheeses and others with *négociants* (traders) whose facilities were at Rungis, the market south of Paris.

Rungis is the market that replaced Les Halles, the vibrant wholesale market in the center of Paris, just west of a neighborhood called the Marais, in the third arrondissement. Les Halles had been for many people the essence of Paris, of France. It was a jumble of buildings with opaque glass windows; of a thick, toxic, stand-still fog from diesel trucks of all sizes and shapes; of bicycle- and scooter-mounted chefs dressed in white and wearing toques; of ill-tended garbage with flies swirling over it, refuse and empty crates and boxes; of rats, cats, and feral dogs. All the produce of France and the rest of Europe was trucked and deposited there—it was the nexus for re-routing the produce to stores, shops, supermarkets, hypermarkets, cafés, and restaurants throughout France and Europe and the rest of the world, a world hungry for French food—Asia, the Middle East, everywhere. But it had long outworn its welcome. Les Halles had to go.

Rungis was a small village in the *banlieue* (suburbs) of Paris that fell victim to the French version of eminent domain. It was flattened in order to create a vast industrial complex, with Quonset huts the size of airplane han-gars: one for fruits and vegetables, one for cheese and dairy products, one for fish and seafood, one for meat and poultry, even one for flowers. I was partic-ularly smitten by the depots for culinary professionals and supermarket and shop operators. Oh, my lord, every cooking tool and implement imaginable was sold there, and at wholesale prices. Michelle and I still use the copper

Ah, Rungis

I thought I had died and gone to heaven. The first thing I ever saw there has imprinted itself on my psyche and serves as my gastronomic psychological gesture, if I may insert a bit of Stanislavski's theory of acting into this narrative. It was around four o'clock one morning in the late 1970s, a cold, dreary, forbidding, windblown, rain-pelted morning, unwelcome to me on this, my first trip out. Commerce commences at Rungis just after midnight six days a week. By seven or eight in the morning, the market is quiet again, except for porters, latecomers, and lategoers. Most of the trucks are long gone or are parked and silent. Having parked my rented car and been admitted (I was required to have a pass, and one had been given to me by one of my cheese merchants), I strolled up to the first gargantuan building, made of corrugated tin like a Quonset hut, its exterior illuminated by a bare light-bulb dangling from a cord attached to an overhang. Beneath this overhang was a pallet on which was a pyramid of recently shot wild boars, each with a wire-hung tag attached to a black back hoof, each tag fluttering in the gloom. These *sangliers* had just been delivered to Rungis from the forests of Dauphiné, the sprawling, mountainous region where the liqueur aperitif Chartreuse is made, just below the Lyonnais and above Provence. I remember those malevolent tusks, those lifeless eyes, the stillness of the carcasses belying the dancing hoof tags. My empathy for the life and death of those beasts was short-lived, though. I could almost smell the wine-dark daube they would become.

pots and pans I dragged home from my visits in the late 1970s and early 1980s. We still use as a dish towel a butcher's cloth I bought back then, a coarsely woven bolt of cotton about two feet by four feet that butchers would tuck into the tie of their apron to sop up blood and gore. I fell for the little blackboards attached to four-inch, sharp-pointed steel pins on which merchants would chalk LE RADIS 2F/BOTTE, or the name and price of whatever else they sold. I was enchanted by the little wooden boxes designed for the storage of cheeses. They were hinge-trapped on top; the four sides were screens; and they were meant to be hung from a tree limb or from the porch, so that while the breezes nourished the cheeses, no fly could get to them. A similar terra-cotta device designed to store butter is, I still think, among the most ingenious items of food hardware of all time: it was a round crock with small holes in it, the upper part crammed with butter and residing upside down in a lower, hollow section that had a quarter inch of water in it so your butter would always be room temperature, cooled by the water, but not oxidized.

I also fell for the cafés at Rungis, all of which were set up expressly for the truck drivers, merchants, and wholesale customers, chefs included. The food they served was not by any means fancy, but as you might expect, it was expertly prepared with impeccable ingredients. All the old classics were de rigueur—pigs' feet, *blanquette de veau, sole meunière,* headcheese, coq au vin. The customers demanded them. We simply have to have a café like one of these at Fairway, I thought to myself—and finally we do, I am proud to say, albeit twenty years later. Mitchel London operates it.

For me, Rungis was a pinnacle and an epiphany. It stood as the measure of all that would give me the strength, endurance, and desire to show up at Fairway for the rest of my professional life. As if seemingly endless rows of every cheese, butter, and egg in France weren't enough, I was also infatuated by the fish, the bivalves, and the crustaceans of every color, size, and species. The rabbits and venison, the quails, partridge, guinea hens, ducks, and geese. The barrels of spices, olives, coffees, and teas. I have visited the commercial markets of many cities since then, but Rungis reigns as the grandest amalgam of foodstuffs I've ever seen anywhere.

There really is no other foodstuff as perfect as cheese—neither fruits nor vegetables, meat nor seafood, beans nor grains, breads nor pastries. Not one of these food groups comes close to the intensity and nuance of flavor and fragrance achieved by cheese, its remarkable gamut of textures, its ambassadorial regional specificity. I love the way cheese gives a happy, welcoming halloo to other foods, as if it's on a mission, a stalwart traveler perfectly content to ride alone but even more ebullient with company. I also love the way cheese acts as the mediator between often quarrelsome tablemates: whiny wine too young to be out this late, a sulkingly bitter olive or almond, a tarted-up, shameless piece of fruit.

No foodstuff is so beckoningly sensuous as cheese. The texture of Vach-

Butterflied Baby Chicken au Poivre

This recipe is a piece of cake, and it's one of Mitchel's favorites. It is fancy without being fussy, and as I say, easy, not to mention highly memorable; and it is likely to become a part of your standard repertoire. It's just the sort of thing you'll find at those little bistros in France.

2 baby chickens, poussins, or Cornish game hens (1 to 1½ pounds each)

¼ cup crushed black peppercorns

Kosher or sea salt, for seasoning

¼ cup heavy cream

1 bunch watercress for garnish (optional)

1. Preheat the oven to 450°F.
2. Cut the breast of each chicken down the middle with kitchen shears or a sharp knife and press it out flat. Rub the chickens on all sides with the crushed peppercorns and salt.
3. Heat a heavy, well-seasoned cast-iron pan over medium-high heat for a few minutes until it is very hot but not smoking. (A cast-iron pan works best for this dish, but a heavy-bottomed frying pan will be fine as long as it can go into the oven.) Place one chicken skin-side down in the hot pan and sear it for about 15 minutes, or until the skin is golden-brown (trust me, it won't stick to the pan once a seared crust has formed). Transfer the chicken to a plate. Repeat with the second chicken.
4. Return both chickens to the pan, skin-side up, and transfer the pan to the oven. Roast for 10 minutes; then remove the pan from the oven and transfer the chickens to heated plates. Do not cover them.
5. Return the pan to the stovetop over medium heat. Pour in the heavy cream to deglaze the pan, scraping up all the browned bits of chicken and stirring them into the sauce. Bring the cream to a boil, stirring; then continue to stir and simmer gently until the cream thickens slightly, 2 to 3 minutes. Pour the cream over the chickens and garnish with a bit of watercress.

Chef's Note: You can grind the pepper coarsely in a peppermill, but we prefer crushing whole peppercorns on a cutting board with the bottom of your heavy cast-iron pan or with the flat of a knife. You can also crush the pepper in a mortar and pestle. You'll get a more varied, interesting texture.

Runny Cheese Potatoes

Serves 4

Sounds good to me. This is a simple precursor to cheese fondue, and I don't know of a better combination with a nice bottle of red wine.

1. Preheat the oven to 350°F. In a saucepan fitted with a steamer, steam the potatoes until they are completely cooked through, about 20 minutes.
2. Divide the potatoes among 4 shallow bowls and sprinkle with sea salt.
3. Warm the wheel of cheese in the oven until it is molten inside but still holds its form, 3 to 6 minutes, depending on size. (You can leave it in the wood box or ceramic pot it came in, but remove all plastic wrap and paper labels.)
4. Spoon the warmed, runny cheese over the steamed potatoes, digging into the center of the wheel first. Serve with the crusty bread, butter, and cornichons.

20 fingerling potatoes, unpeeled, the smallest you can find (about 1 pound)

Coarse sea salt, for serving

1 wheel Vacherin Mont d'Or or Saint-Marcellin cheese, very ripe (see Cheesemonger's Note)

1 loaf crusty bread, sliced, for serving

Unsalted butter, for serving

½ pint cornichons, for serving

Cheesemonger's Note: You are by no means limited to Swiss or French Vacherin Mont d'Or and the Rhone Valley's Saint-Marcellin (though these are two of my absolute favorite cheeses). Without hesitation, consider also French Munster d'Alsace, a whole two-pound wheel; also, the magnificent raw sheep's milk Spanish Extremaduran Torta del Casar, as well as Saint-Marcellin's sister cheese from nearby Saint-Félicien, farther west across the Rhône, which is identical in taste, though larger. The great Savoie cheese reblochon would be wonderful, too.

I would remove the crust (which, in texture, is like the velvety covering of deer antlers) from just the top of the reblochon and figure on two of the one-pound wheels for four people. The Munster and the Torta will serve four to six, but the Saint-Marcellins are tiny—you'll need one per person. Three Saint-Féliciens will feed four. You're best off removing the top crust from the Vacherin and the Torta before heating, but don't bother removing the rind from any of the others.

John Creedilmor and Katie Mitchell,
Broadway cheese counter stalwarts.

Fromage de chèvre
au Lait Pasteurisé
Le Cabri d'Antan
20 pour cent
de matière grasse
sur poids total
Poids Net à
l'emballage
200g
FR
79.184.01
CE
Fabriqué en Poitou

erin Mont d'Or is voluptuous. In dominatrix fashion, each is belted by a strip of highly aromatic Norwegian spruce bark, lest she spill out of her costume. The feminine chèvre Sainte-Maure de Touraine is hermaphroditically phallic, and even pierced with a piece of rye straw from end to end to keep it from falling to pieces. A true Camembert smells of sex. Numerous cheeses have been named for and made to resemble the female breast. The arousal of every cheese by brief exposure to room temperature is evidenced when the cheese becomes moist and slippery. (Cheese as an elegant and traditional coda to haute cuisine? As you wish. For me, I prefer it down and dirty.)

And yet cheese is low-maintenance. I value the fact that it requires little more than one's knife and a sturdy surface. Nor is it balefully evanescent like fruit and flesh. It will be there when you need it.

My heavens, the enormous array of cheeses to choose from is overwhelming. People are entitled to like what they like, but the matter really comes down to a few simple questions, if you'll indulge me for a moment. (I'd prefer that you indulge me for a lifetime, but let's start with a moment.)

Is the cheese made more by a person, or by a machine? Cheese tools are one thing. Even the most hands-on cheese recipe requires vats, hoses, rakes, colanders, and thermometers. But if a cheese is a product of an assembly line, where very soon the few humans still involved will be replaced by robotic arms, then I say, "No thanks!"

Has the cheese been made from raw milk? To use pasteurized milk in the creation of a cheese is unthinkable, illogical, if in fact the goal is to make a cheese that is as good as it can possibly be. And there can be no other goal than that, for me, for all of us.

Does the cheese look good and give itself up nobly to the knife? Cheese making and cheese constitute one of the few areas in life where you can judge a book by its cover. I don't even need to taste a cheese to know whether it's good or not. If I behold a cheese that looks as if it just stepped out of a limousine rather than a truck, a cheese wearing a three-piece suit rather than flannel and corduroy, I will not select it. A cheese whose exterior is flaw-less and glossy almost certainly promises to have an interior that is flabby and slablike. It is not worthy.

If, on the other hand, I behold an exterior in some natural shade; if it has a toadlike skin or a pebbly surface or deer antlers' velvet, a surface that begs to be stroked or is cloaked in gray gingham or is stippled or tattooed over every square inch with its name and provenance; if it is dusted or rouged or cobwebbed with some beneficent mold; or if it, like *fermier* (farm-made) Saint-Nectaire, looks like an expressionist painting or a Hubble telescope photograph of a distant galaxy, reflecting the white, yellow, red, green, and black of five distinct strains of wild yeasts, each a healthy, flavor-producing substance—I then know the cheese is going to taste good. Heaven knows it looks good. As for that business about the knife, don't worry about it. It will cut just fine.

You see, artisanal cheeses have natural rinds—crusts that have oc-curred naturally, as a cardinally important part of the artisanal recipe. Their exteriors are earth tones, from bone-white to beige to khaki to straw through the russet reds, rawhides, and chocolaty browns. Sometimes, like several of

the great British cheeses, Cheddars and Cheshires among them, they are wrapped in cloth, usually cotton gingham. Rarely are they smooth on the outside—they're often mottled, often pebbly, often dusted with some strain or strains of natural yeasts and molds that contribute their own flavors to the ripening and finished cheese. These rinds are either edible or not, a simple matter of common sense.

Factory-made, mass-produced cheeses have rinds, crusts, that are painted or covered with paper, aluminum foil, plastic, or—worse—wax. These are essentially cheeses in burkas. Without the rinds that occur naturally—often helped along by brushing, buffing, rubbing, or "washing" (direct application of liquid at intervals by hand or by using a cloth or a brush, be the liquid water or beer, wine or brine, or some spirit or secret spice- or herb-infused concoction)—a cheese cannot evolve. Wrapping, painting, or waxing cuts off the beautiful life of a cheese. It is a calculated swap in order to create a sort of unnatural stasis, in order to extend its shelf life as long as possible, with no eye toward its progress from good to better to best.

The hidden truth is that the exterior defines the cheese and from a cheesemaker's standpoint is as important as the interior. Cheese rinds are the equivalent of your skin, arguably the most important organ of the body. Skin houses and protects all the other moving and working parts and organs, and it enables the body as a whole—just like a cheese—to breathe. Without it, nothing would work.

Soft cheeses such as Brie and Camembert ripen from the outside, with its natural bloomy rind, to the inside. These days insipid, factory-made soft-ripened cheeses are manufactured by the thousands of tons, as compared with the piddling quantities of artisanal soft-ripened varieties. In order to obviate the nettlesome necessity for mass-produced Brie or Camembert or Chaource to ripen naturally, the curd that will become those cheeses is subjected to a "washing," which removes whatever proteins, caseins, and flavor-evolving bacteria have somehow managed to survive the brutal pasteurization process. It is a means of relieving the retailer of a problem: having only

x amount of time to sell a product while approximating (somewhat) the texture, color, and flavor of the cheese it is meant to imitate.

So look at the exterior of a cheese. If it is encased in some artificial substance and reflects a bright primary or secondary color, reject it out of hand. Likewise, if it sports a label in a bright primary color with a logo crafted by a committee, it is obviously a product of big-budget marketing.

A Guide to Your Favorite Cheeses

Don't know the name, but know what you like? Choose from the categories below.

Fresh and Fluffy

Délice de Bourgogne, Délice de Pommard, Jean Grogne, Pierre Robert, Gratte-Paille, Saint André, Brillat-Savarin, Explorateur, Chaource, Can Pujol, *burrata, mozzarella di bufala,* any fresh chèvre (such as Cornilly, Selles-sur-Cher, Valençay, Petit Billy, Pointe de Bique, Picandou), Humboldt Fog, La Tur (Piedmont goat Robiola)

Creamy and Dreamy

Chevrol, Florette, Berger de Rocastin, Camembert le Rustique, Edel de Cléron, Duo de Brie with Gorgonzola, Roucoulons, Pérail (Lou Pérac), Marzolino (Pecorino Toscano), Coach Farm Triple-Cream

Strong and Gooshy

Munster d'Alsace, Saint-Marcellin, Saint-Félicien, Langres, Affidelice Berthaut, Epoisses Berthaut, Le Châtelain Camembert, Brie Rouzaire, Camembert d'Isigny, Gorgonzola Dolce, Stinking Bishop, Livarot, Pont-l'Evêque, reblochon, Serpa (Portugal), Serra da Estrela (Portugal), Azeitão (Portugal), Vacherin Mont d'Or, Torta del Casar, Queso de la Serena

Supple and Intense

Abondance, aged Comté, Beaufort, Saint-Nectaire, Le Brouère, Mahón, Cantal, Bethmale, Bethmale Chèvre, Brézain, Fournols, Morbier, Chimay, Le Pavin, Vacherin Fribourgeois, Grafton Cheddar, Pleasant Ridge Reserve, Fontina d'Aosta, Mont-des-Cats, Tomme de Savoie, Tomme de Yenne

Hard and Not So Sharp

Moulis Brebis, Moulis Chèvre, Erhaki, Mimolette, Onetik, Ossau-Iraty, Manchego, Roncal, Idiazábal, Garrotxa, Moliterno, Rossellino (Pecorino Toscano), Corsignano (Pecorino Toscano), Pecorino in Foglie di Noce, Mrs. Appleby's Cheshire, Mrs. Kirkham's Lancashire, Keen's and Montgomery's Cheddars, Farmhouse Leicester, Vermont Shepherd's Cheese

Hard and Sharp

Tête de Moine, Appenzeller, Majorero, Provolone, Parmigiano-Reggiano, Grana Padano, Pecorino Romano, Sicilian Pepato, aged Boerenkaas, Dutch Parrano, California Dry Jack, São Jorge (Azores-Portugal), Pecorino di Fossa

True Blue

Stilton, Shropshire Blue, Basque Bleu, Bleu d'Auvergne, Fourme d'Ambert, Bleu de Gex, Roquefort, aged (*stagionato*) Gorgonzola, Cabrales, Picón, Rogue River Bleu, Great Hill Blue, Bingham Hill Blue, Berkshire Blue

Bland and Forgettable

Pasteurized Brie, Herb Brie, Pepper Brie, Royal Camembert, red wax Gouda, Havarti, yogurt cheese, Monterey Jack, Cacio di Roma, Saga Blue, Cambozola, Doux de Montagne, string cheese, diet cheeses (Swiss Lorraine, etc.), Jarlsberg, Drunken Goat

9

My Department Grows by
Leaps and Bounds

So I got the cheeses I wanted—400 or so—for my department, but they weren't the half of it. I physically grew my department by stacking standard milk crates three high and covering them with a material like Astroturf. On this new real estate, which over the ensuing years increased my merchandisable space incrementally until I ran out of floor, I laid out noncheese items that were close to cheese, that went with cheese, that were tangential to cheese within the realm of gastronomy.

Among my then unusual items that were cheese, or close to it, was mascarpone—which must not be called a cheese. It's Lombardy's heavy cream, acidulated with lemon juice in order to separate all its moisture from it, leaving behind a sort of sweet, blond pudding. I stocked farmer cheese and baked farmer cheese with fruit or scallion in it, and pot cheese, which is basically bulk cottage cheese, but drier. I had *bocconcini* ("little mouthfuls") and *ciliegine* ("little cherries") of fresh, handmade mozzarella dressed with chopped parsley, garlic, hot red chile flakes, and extra-virgin olive oil. There were six or eight kinds of feta (which means "slice"), the only cheese, really, for many, many people. We offered feta right out of the 100-pound brine-filled wooden barrel. These are all specialty dairy products that simply couldn't have survived in the retail arena if they were merchandised with the standard dairy product mix, at least not in the early days. They had to be coddled and cosseted within the confines of the cheese specialist. These days they're staples, but back then, in the few shops such as Fairway that made them available, they were genuinely special.

I was wildly into wild mushrooms before any of the city's chefs and certainly before anyone at the other higher-end food shops, and I brought them into my department. Howie's wife, Nita, was in the basket business, so I had a wealth of basketry to choose from. I had baskets overflowing with black and beige morels (the black morels have a more intense flavor); chanterelles (a word that always sounds French to me, though it isn't—the name comes from the Latin for the apricot-colored, amazingly apricot-fragrant chanterelle, *cantherellus,* and the French term for the mushroom is *girolle,* which means a sort of ruffle); black trumpets (*trompettes de la mort*—ominous-sounding, though perhaps my favorite mushroom of all); hedgehogs and cauliflower mushrooms in clumps bigger than your head; the meaty hen-of-the-woods; the rather insipid yellow-foot chanterelles; slippery, greasy wood ears; scrumptious oyster mushrooms; shiitakes; and other more common "wild" varieties such as cremini and portobello, in those days still found in the wild, not yet wild-cultivated as they are today. You can imagine how beautiful this area was, how compelling and well-nigh irresistible to New Yorkers infatuated with food and

PREVIOUS SPREAD, LEFT:
The Upper West Side (Broadway and 74th Street) store, the flagship.

Two Cucumber and Cheese Salads

Each serves 4

These are so refreshing and so good to serve with a simple meal (toasted bagels, cream cheese, and smoked salmon, for instance; or turkey sandwiches; or burgers). Or just grab a baguette and sit down to a big plate of cucumbers and cheese and call it lunch. The cheese is the star ingredient here, so consult your cheesemonger and get something nice.

Cucumber and Feta Salad

1 hothouse cucumber (also known as an English cucumber), peeled to create stripes on the outside and sliced into rounds

2 tablespoons extra-virgin olive oil (the best quality you can find)

Freshly ground black pepper, to taste

¼ red onion, very thinly sliced (on a mandoline if available)

¾ pound feta cheese, cubed

Kosher or sea salt, optional

2 tablespoons chopped flat-leaf parsley

1. In a medium bowl, toss the cucumber with the olive oil and season with pepper. Add the onion and toss again.
2. Add the cubed feta and toss gently, taking care not to break the cubes of cheese. Taste and season with salt if desired (this will depend on the saltiness of the feta).
3. I always want to add a teaspoonful of red wine vinegar here, but my wife disagrees, so . . . garnish with the parsley and serve.

Cucumber and Chèvre Salad

1 hothouse cucumber (also known as an English cucumber), peeled to create stripes on the outside and sliced into rounds

1 tablespoon fresh lemon juice

Kosher or sea salt and freshly ground black pepper, to taste

6 ounces semi-aged chèvre log (such as a Sainte-Maure), sliced into rounds

2 tablespoons extra-virgin olive oil (the best quality you can find)

1 tablespoon chopped chives, for garnish

1. In a shallow serving bowl, lightly toss the sliced cucumber with the lemon juice. Season with salt and pepper.
2. Lay slices of chèvre on top of the cucumber slices and drizzle with olive oil. Garnish with the chives.

Chef's Note: If you're worried about your cucumbers getting soggy—let's say you're preparing this dish for a buffet, and it won't be consumed right away—you might want to use this technique for crisping them before adding them to your salad. Arrange the cucumber slices in a colander placed inside a bowl. Sprinkle with salt, cover with ice cubes, and refrigerate for 1 hour. Pat dry and use. Remember to reduce or eliminate the salt in your recipe if you use this technique.

Roasted Shiitake Mushrooms

Serves 4

This is a great, peasantlike first course that always elicits oohs and ahhs. You can roast any mushroom like this—you're not limited to shiitake, by any means. But Colette famously swore that the champignon de Paris (the ordinary button mushroom) would never cross her hearth as long as she lived, and I'm not sure I don't agree. Button mushrooms are about as thrilling as tofu, as far as I'm concerned. When I have my druthers, the mushroom I choose is *Boletus edulis* (aka the *porcino,* the *cèpe,* the *Steinpilze*), the most flavorful mushroom there is. (Don't let people tell you it's the matsutake; it isn't.) But fresh porcini cost a fortune, and roasting shiitake this way brings out incredible flavor. Sprinkle these flat, floppy caps with sea salt when they're sizzling hot, and prepare to fall to your knees. Remove your hat. Show some respect.

¼ cup extra-virgin olive oil

1 pound shiitake mushrooms, stems removed

10 garlic cloves, lightly crushed (skins on)

8 sprigs fresh thyme

Kosher or sea salt and freshly ground black pepper, to taste

2 tablespoons chopped flat-leaf parsley, for garnish

1. Preheat the oven to 400°F.
2. In a large, shallow ovenproof frying pan or skillet, heat the olive oil over high heat. Add the shiitake mushrooms and toss to coat with oil. Add the garlic, thyme, salt, and pepper and cook, stirring occasionally, for 5 minutes.
3. Transfer the pan to the oven and roast until the mushrooms are tender and starting to crisp around the edges, 15 to 20 minutes. Sprinkle the mushrooms with parsley and serve.

Grocer's Note: They're called wild mushrooms, and they taste quite wild, but shiitakes are actually the second most cultivated mushroom in the world (they're mostly grown in the United States and Japan). Shiitake stems are the culinary equivalent of baling twine. Discard them. Before throwing them out, however, you could boil them in soup to leach out any flavor they may be harboring.

cooking. More waist-high merchandising space I gave over to baskets of filled pasta.

My closest business friend, Lou Todaro, was my biggest and most important supplier. Lou was morphing from being a food retailer (Todaro Brothers, 2nd Avenue at 30th Street in Manhattan) to being an importer and distributor. He was a first-generation New Yorker; his mom and dad came from Caltabellotta, a village in southwestern Sicily. Lou came up with a pasta maker in Bologna. Now, Bologna is not just the capital city of the most significant food region in all of Italy—Emilia-Romagna, origin of Parmigiano-Reggiano, prosciutto di Parma, balsamic vinegar, Lambrusco wine, mortadella, and on and on. It is also the home of tortellini, tortelloni, agnolotti, and cappelletti. So in addition to the cheeses, in addition to the wild mushrooms (oh, and the spring ramps and fiddleheads, which I had before anybody knew they existed—remember, this was the early 1980s, and ramps and fiddleheads didn't become fashionable until, good lord, the late 1990s or the early 2000s), I laid out baskets overflowing with fat, funny little bundles of pasta

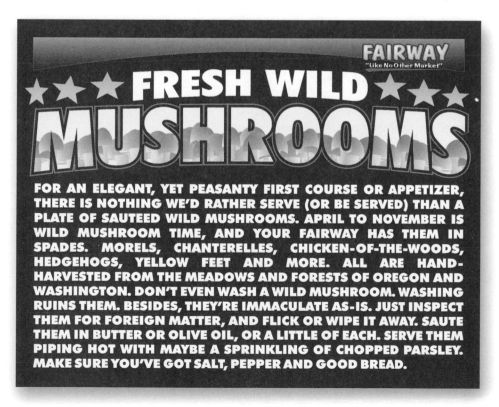

FAIRWAY
"Like No Other Market"

★ ★ ★ FRESH WILD ★ ★ ★
MUSHROOMS

FOR AN ELEGANT, YET PEASANTY FIRST COURSE OR APPETIZER, THERE IS NOTHING WE'D RATHER SERVE (OR BE SERVED) THAN A PLATE OF SAUTEED WILD MUSHROOMS. APRIL TO NOVEMBER IS WILD MUSHROOM TIME, AND YOUR FAIRWAY HAS THEM IN SPADES. MORELS, CHANTERELLES, CHICKEN-OF-THE-WOODS, HEDGEHOGS, YELLOW FEET AND MORE. ALL ARE HAND-HARVESTED FROM THE MEADOWS AND FORESTS OF OREGON AND WASHINGTON. DON'T EVEN WASH A WILD MUSHROOM. WASHING RUINS THEM. BESIDES, THEY'RE IMMACULATE AS-IS. JUST INSPECT THEM FOR FOREIGN MATTER, AND FLICK OR WIPE IT AWAY. SAUTE THEM IN BUTTER OR OLIVE OIL, OR A LITTLE OF EACH. SERVE THEM PIPING HOT WITH MAYBE A SPRINKLING OF CHOPPED PARSLEY. MAKE SURE YOU'VE GOT SALT, PEPPER AND GOOD BREAD.

filled with Gorgonzola, with porcini mushrooms, with ricotta and spinach, with pumpkin and nutmeg, just to name a few. My customers stood in line to shovel their choices into paper sacks that would be weighed and priced for them at my counter or at checkout.

My signs were strict. You were forbidden to pour any idiotic red pasta sauce from a jar over any of these pastas. After cooking (a scant eight to ten minutes), you were instructed to toss the tortellini (or whatever) in a sauce of butter, olive oil, and garlic and then to add a copious amount of freshly grated Parmigiano (or some other preparation). I even stipulated the correct bread to serve with the pasta. I don't care that Italians rarely serve bread with pasta, or indeed with any main course at *cena*.

One real oddball pasta I championed was a dried, fettuccine-size flat noodle made of buckwheat called pizzoccheri ("peet-SOAK-er-ree"), a specialty of the Valtellina area of Lombardy. Ages old, this particular pasta also gives its name to the definitive recipe for it. You cook it as you would regular durum semolina wheat pasta—undercook it a bit, actually. Then it is drained, and in a nice-size baking dish or pan that has been rubbed liberally with butter and garlic, you layer the buckwheat pasta with cooked chard (often referred to as Swiss chard), cooked potatoes, chopped red onion, a few leaves of fresh sage, and finally shredded fontina, the great raw cow's milk cheese of

Piedmont's subregion Aosta. (A well-known cheese from nearby, called Bitto, is similar and is often used in this dish.) Some recipes for pizzoccheri call for spinach instead of chard, but my wife, Michelle, and I are always looking for excuses to use chard rather than just cooking it and serving it with rice, beans, and hot sauces as we so often do. The pizzoccheri is then baked in the oven with or without a dusting of grated Parmigiano, which can be added at the table. This is a scrumptious dish and to me always tastes even better—like lasagna—reheated on subsequent days.

Another pasta dish Michelle adapted from a book by Marcella Hazan and put into her repertoire gave me the opportunity to sell from a basket a lot of orecchiette ("little ears"), a meal that may sound boring but, believe me, is not. Cauliflower is steamed and then broken into chunks and put into a pan with olive oil, chopped garlic, and a few chopped fillets of anchovies. (I'll obsess on anchovies directly—they are very important to me.) Before the cauliflower burns, Michelle shakes a liberal quantity of hot red chile flakes over it, and then combines the whole thing with the cooked orecchiette. Once again, this dish makes a superb leftover, even cold.

I didn't discover the worth of serious anchovies until I began to travel in Spain, and it wasn't until around 2000 that I began to import the best of them. I had been taught that the "best" anchovies came from fishermen-processors on the south coast of Sicily (Sciacca) who would gut them and then pack them in tins and wooden boxes with a lot of sea salt. You had to split them in half with your fingers, pick away as many of the confounded bones as you possibly could, and then soak them in about a dozen baths of cold water in order to wash away the salt. The result was an anchovy fillet that was bony, scaly, fishy, and so salty that it was well-nigh inedible. Because—despite all the information handed down by cookbooks and chefs—it is *not* a cinch to wash the salt off salted anchovies! And it is a myth that serious foodies opt only for salted anchovies. They're going to be irretrievably salty *and*

bony *and* scaly, no matter how much you fuss with them! Luckily, in the late 1990s I was fortunate enough to fall in with a few Spaniards and Catalans who set me straight.

Likewise, forget about supermarket tinned anchovies. Forget about the anchovies used in pizza parlors. They're a vile misrepresentation of one of our greatest culinary gifts. They taste like salty fish guts, whereas serious anchovies taste like adult candy. They are indispensable for stews, for daubes, for soups, and for innumerable pasta dishes. To prove this, sit before a couple of fillets packed in olive oil, from companies such as Roque (Collioure, France), Ortiz (Pays Vasco, Spain), and Recca (Sciacca, Sicily). Try, for example, l'Escala anchovies, preserved in olive oil in jars, wood-fire-roasted, hand-filleted,

hand-packed. They come from l'Escala, the famous old fishing village on the Catalan coast north of Barcelona, almost to the French Catalan international border, a glorious and wondrous place, not far from the stunning Greek and Roman ruins at Empúries. Along with my Roque anchovies from Collioure, just up the coast, they are the ultimate. What else do you need? A handful of marcona almonds. A glass of cold fino sherry. Crusty bread. The lights will go on for you. Now you know.

I really shouldn't fail to mention the snails I had in my department. For several months in those early days of importing, I had baskets like wicker laundry hampers filled to the brim with *petit-gris*, little gray snails, called *lumache* or *chiocciole* or *babaluci*, from Sicily. I found them at the Brooklyn

OPPOSITE:
The Red Hook, Brooklyn, store.

Pasta with Cauliflower, Golden Raisins, and Anchovies

Serves 4

The "white" anchovies, or *boquerones,* called for in this recipe are especially good. They've been pickled in white wine vinegar rather than having been cured in salt, and the vinegar retains more of their natural silvery color and their delicate flavor.

2 tablespoons golden raisins

2 tablespoons pine nuts

1 tablespoon plus 1 teaspoon kosher or sea salt

1 head cauliflower, trimmed into florets, core and stem discarded

½ cup extra-virgin olive oil, plus additional, as needed

3 garlic cloves, peeled and sliced as thinly as possible

8 anchovies, preferably white anchovies (see Chef's Note), broken up roughly

Freshly ground black pepper to taste

1 pound dried gemelli pasta or spaghetti

Roughly chopped flat-leaf parsley leaves, for garnish

Coarsely grated Parmesan, for serving

1. Place the raisins in a bowl, cover them with hot water, and let soak until plump, about 15 minutes. Drain and set aside. In a dry, heavy-bottom skillet over medium heat, toast the pine nuts until pale golden, about 2 minutes. Set aside.

2. Bring 6 quarts of water to a rolling boil and add 1 tablespoon of salt. Place the cauliflower florets in a large mesh strainer and immerse the strainer in the boiling water. Blanch them for about 8 minutes. You want to save the cooking water for the pasta, so using a strainer makes taking the cauliflower from the water simple and quick. If you don't have a strainer, remove the florets using a slotted spoon. Set the blanched cauliflower aside. Keep the water at a simmer.

3. In a large, deep skillet, heat the olive oil over low heat and add the garlic, sautéing slowly until it just starts to become golden, about 2 minutes. Add the cauliflower, raise the heat to medium, and sauté for 5 minutes. Add the anchovies, raisins, and toasted pine nuts. Reduce the heat to medium-low, stir, and continue cooking until the anchovies start to dissolve into the oil and the cauliflower is tender, about 5 minutes more. Season with ½ teaspoon kosher or sea salt and freshly ground black pepper.

4. Meanwhile, return the cooking water to a boil and add the pasta. Cook according to package directions for al dente (firm to the bite). Drain the pasta and add it to the cauliflower sauce. Toss the pasta over medium heat until thoroughly warmed. Transfer it to a warmed serving bowl or individual plates. Garnish with the parsley leaves and serve with grated Parmesan.

Chef's Note: If you can't find white anchovies, use the best imported anchovy fillets available in a tin or a jar. Keep in mind that these are generally cured in salt before being packed in olive oil and are consequently a lot saltier than those classified as white, so adjust your seasoning accordingly.

Terminal Market, a local produce distribution center. All you had to do was boil, broil, or grill them and then, say, add them to a sauce or a gratin, or just serve them cooked with a sauce of butter and garlic. With a pin you tap a little hole in the shell and then suck out the creature, and it is delicious. But these snails were alive—very much alive; we had to keep the lid on the hamper or in a matter of minutes they would be like, "Hi-ho, hi-ho, it's off to work we go." But there were a lot more than seven of these dwarfs, more like 7,000. That idea of a "snail's pace" must apply to another species. I chose to sell them in the cheese department so I could keep an eye on them. For a while there, we sent a lot of people home with a nice hunk of cheese wrapped up (inadvertently) with a snail or two. Several elementary school teachers who were regulars at Fairway bought snails to take to their classrooms as pets. Those snails lived for years, and Fairway was a hero to these teachers and students.

The Red Hook, Brooklyn, store.

10

Olives Are Beautiful

Sometime in the early 1980s I came home to New York from a trip to France particularly smitten with the way olives were sold there. (I can't remember where I was when it dawned on me that New Yorkers hadn't a clue about olives. I was in Provence. I'm sure I'd flown down to Marseille from Paris and rented a car. Maybe I was at a street market in Avignon.) I had always been inordinately fond of olives, but I didn't know much about them.

Growing up, all I was aware of was that they came from Mom's Safeway to her pantry. The black ones came in cans, and the pimiento-stuffed green ones came in jars. Nobody in our house drank martinis, so I guess Mom had olives around for the neighbors and friends who did, and for her potato salads and deviled eggs. The black ones were pitted. You remember them. You take four of them, stick one on each of the fingers of one hand, wave a wiggling bye-bye to yourself, and then eat them. I loved the liquid they left behind. Many were the times I'd pass by the refrigerator and have a don't-mind-if-I-do swig right from the can. It was just as good as maraschino cherry juice.

That was the sum total of my knowledge of olives.

Once I began paying attention, it took me almost no time to notice that olives are beautiful. Later, I learned that olive trees are beautiful, too. George Orwell once said that if he had another lifetime to live, he would spend it painting pictures of nothing but olive trees.

My brainstorm was that olives are just like any other salad ingredient in that they need to be washed and then dressed. But nobody I knew understood that: in Manhattan's Little Italy, not even one operator of a *salumeria, latteria,* or Italian grocery—and not even one of Brooklyn's Middle Eastern food shop proprietors on Atlantic Avenue. And all those stores sold tons of olives, many of them in bulk rather than in cans and jars. New Yorkers would dump olives from whatever container they came in directly into a dish and put it on the table. When you eat olives served like that, all you're going to taste is the saltiness. No wonder so many people in those days were indifferent to olives. Even today, otherwise food-savvy people can be heard to say they don't like olives, and that's why. They've never tasted an olive that has been treated with respect. All olives should be washed in cold water and gently bounced dry. They've been soaking in brine for months, for heaven's sake.

I also learned that every olive-producing region in Europe special-izes in certain varieties that differ more in shape and size than in color or flavor, and that each variety is always dressed in a specific fashion, as you will soon see.

I further learned that those California-grown, bland, black, finger puppet olives are as phony as can be. They were green before they got the good old American treatment. Jets of oxygen are injected into a vigorous, days-long lye bath, which not only extracts all the bitter glucosides that render an uncured olive inedible, unpalatable, much the way an acorn tastes, but also serves to oxidize the green olive and turn it black. Ripe olives of this manzanilla or mission variety are actually dark red or purple when they are left on the tree past their young green stage. These so-called black olives have been so processed, so robbed of any vestige of oliveness, that what is left is hardly an olive at all. There's nothing left but texture, just as with black or white truffles from a tin or a jar. The liquid they're packed in has more flavor than the item itself. Nota bene: truffles from a jar or a tin are but a cosmetic. Chefs use them to decorate foods like poultry and terrines of foie gras. Save your money for fresh truffles in season.

Those California-grown green stuffed olives are not exactly distinguished, either. That little strip of pimiento? Part of it—but not much—may have started out a member of the genus *Capsicum* (chile peppers). The red thing's origin aside, what is machine-inserted into that little olive is something that was off-stand produce to begin with—cracked, bruised, overripe, undersize, whatever—and so was sold to the olive processor who chopped it, mulched it, pureed it, combined it with preservatives and dye, played some other arcane machine tricks on the entire mass, and finally extruded it from yet another machine into an unending ribbon of the desired hue of crimson so it could be cut into precise lengths according to the size of the green olive it was about to violate.

I decided that my cheese counter needed to sell proper olives. They are a perfect accompaniment to many, many cheeses, and I feel strongly that olives go best with cheeses made in the same regions that grow the olives. Hardly any olives are grown in regions where cattle predominate, so it makes sense to me that cow's milk cheese is just not right with olives. They taste better with cheese made from the milk of sheep and goats, which thrive in areas noted for their olives—much of Greece, for example. Greeks make a lot of yogurt from cow's milk, but no cow's milk cheese to speak of. The same goes for southern Italy, which is blanketed with olive groves—with the exception of *mozzarella di bufala,* which is made from the milk of water buffalo (*bufala*); *fior di latte* (mozzarella made from cow's milk); and caciocavallo and provolone. Sheep's milk reigns supreme in southern Italy, and in southern and southwestern France. There are a lot of cows in southwestern France, but sheep predominate. Spain has plenty of cattle, but a lot more sheep and goats. I can think of only a few Spanish cow's milk cheeses—Mahón from Minorca (no olives) in the Balearic Islands (Majorca, Ibiza, Formentera), Afuega'l Pitu from Asturias (no olives) in the north. An obscure though important name-controlled Catalan cheese, l'Alt Urgell y Cerdanya (lots of olives, but then, lots of goats and sheep, too); and a couple of snorers from Galicia (no olives), San Simón and Tetilla. The great Azores cheese São Jorge (Saint George) is made from cow's milk, but that's an anomaly—cows showed up there only because these Portuguese islands were a vital replenishing stop on the sixteenth-century Atlantic maritime trade route, as were Madeira and the Canary Islands (named not for little yellow birds, but for the dogs—*cane*—that escaped from ships or were abandoned by heartless sailors).

STEVE'S BLOG OF THE DAY
July 22, 2006

Visited Extremadura (Almendralejo, to be exact, not far from Cáceres) to see my olive brothers in March, and it took the two bumblers till now to furnish us with six pallets of their glorious olives. Anchovy-flavored manzanillas and lemon-flavored manzanillas. OK, sounds gross, an olive macerated in anchovy guts. I remind you that *garum*, the cherished sauce created by the Romans 2,000 or 3,000 years ago, was the original mayonnaise, peanut butter, *chimichurri*, and ketchup all fermented into one. Place fish guts in an earthenware urn; place urn in sun, uncovered. Wait until bubbly and foul. Pour off liquid. Bottle. Use unsparingly on everything. These anchovy olives should be developed into a chewing gum. God almighty, they're good. So are the lemon-flavored ones.

That's about it. Even in Portugal, where the olives and olive oil are sublime, all the cheeses—and stunningly delicious they are—are made from goat's milk and sheep's milk.

The first olive I decided to wash, dress, and sell was the cracked Sicilian. "Cracked" refers to the fact that the olives are actually whacked so they'll cure faster. Well, many are slit with a knife, by hand, but some to this day are bludgeoned with a brick or mallet. The faster the olives cure, the sooner the processor gets his money. But I digress.

Cracked Sicilians are green olives. A Sicilian style of dressing them is to first wash them to rid them of their saltiness. Then, according to however much you have chosen to dress, you crush cloves or entire heads of garlic. I put the garlic on a clean cloth, fold over a length of the cloth, and then beat the garlic with a mallet or a rolling pin. If I haven't peeled the garlic, I'll pick away some of the parchment without getting too fastidious about it. Next, I do the same thing with a quantity of fresh, hot red and green chiles.

Picadillo

This much-loved, hearty beef stew with olives, capers, tomatoes, peppers, and plenty of vinegar is a Spanish New World classic. Cubans serve it with rice and beans. Mexicans stuff things with it. For the olives, I recommend Moroccan oil-cured. Leave the pits in, and just warn your diners.

3 tablespoons extra-virgin olive oil

2 medium onions, finely chopped

1 large bell pepper, finely chopped

1 to 2 jalapeño peppers (to taste), finely chopped, seeds removed if desired

2 pounds lean ground beef (or 1 pound each lean ground beef and ground pork or turkey)

6 plum tomatoes, seeded and chopped

1 small garlic clove, finely chopped

2 teaspoons ground cumin

2 teaspoons ground coriander

½ to 1 teaspoon cayenne, to taste

Kosher or sea salt and freshly ground black pepper, to taste

½ cup balsamic vinegar

½ cup tomato puree

¼ cup chopped ripe olives (black oil-cured Moroccans, pitted taggiasca, or Niçoise)

2 tablespoons capers, rinsed and drained

Bibb or iceberg lettuce leaves or steamed white rice, for serving (optional)

1. Heat the olive oil in a large skillet over medium heat. Add the onion, bell pepper, and jalapeño peppers. Cook until browned, about 10 minutes. Add the meat and stir, breaking it up into tiny pieces with a wooden spoon, until browned, about 10 minutes. Stir in the tomatoes, garlic, cumin, coriander, cayenne, and salt and pepper, and cook, stirring, until fragrant, about 2 minutes.

2. Stir in the vinegar, tomato puree, olives, and capers and bring the stew to a boil. Reduce the heat and simmer, stirring occasionally, for 1 hour. Serve in Bibb or iceberg lettuce cups or over steamed white rice, if desired.

Grocer's Note: Salted capers, preferably the Italian variety from Pantelleria (a tiny island between Sicily and Libya), taste immensely more interesting, since they haven't been watered down in brine or vinegar. Bounce them in a colander under the cold tap to wash away the salt, and then pat them dry with a paper towel or cloth.

Jalapeños work fine, though any hot chile will do. In fact, although I prefer fresh chiles, dried hot red chile flakes are good, too, if that's what you've got.

You're finished. Just combine the garlic and the chiles and the olives in a bowl and cover the whole thing with extra-virgin olive oil. The oil will be infused with the heat and flavor from the chile and garlic, and the fact that the olives are cracked all the way to the pit ensures that they'll absorb the flavors more rapidly and more intensely. And don't think of the olive oil as merely a delivery system, a foil for the chile and garlic. You have now created an *olio santo*, "sanctified oil," a splendid and requisite Italian table condiment for all kinds of foods.

Traditionally, *olio santo* is merely a bottle or cruet of olive oil in which hot chiles and often other herbs and spices (oregano, peppercorns) have been allowed to macerate. This spicy-hot concoction is dribbled over everything— pizza, toast, rice, potatoes, fish and other seafood, meats and poultry, cooked vegetables. Ligurian Italians make a spicy-hot oil such as this that they call *pinzimonio*. It can serve as a meal when raw and cooked vegetables and shards of bread are provided to be dipped into the mixture.

But back to the cracked Sicilians. I like to use as robust an olive oil as possible—in this case, logically, a western Sicilian of a particular provenance and variety (biancolilla), unfiltered. Again, the filtering of olive oil is a cosmetic blandishment. Somebody somewhere sometime decided that olive oil should be crystal-clear. That's just great. Let's all sacrifice fragrance and flavor for clarity.

These dressed cracked Sicilians are delicious and as agreeable with cocktails, particularly vodka and gin, as they are with wines, cheeses, salumi, and bread. I started out selling them by putting them in a large stoneware bowl that held about six pounds, and they quickly became a fixture at the counter.

In fact, it was a constant struggle to keep the damn bowl full. Not to mention that I began to sell so much of the *olio santo* that I had to prepare and bottle it separately. So I added another olive: the Gaeta, a midsize purple olive that is neither large like the cracked Sicilian nor tiny like an arbequina from Catalonia nor huge like one of the many outsize green olives.

Gaeta ("gah-EH-ta") is a peninsular town on the west coast of Italy on the Tyrrhenian Sea just up the coast from Naples toward Rome. Olive groves have been cultivated there since before Christ's time. The olive oil is good—though nothing to write home about—but the cured olives are delicious: meaty, nutty, as good as can be. They've always had a following in New York because so many Italian New Yorkers came here from southern Italy. The Gaeta olive has been a staple for them.

Like the dressed cracked Sicilians, my Gaetas were also an immediate hit. After washing and drying them, I combined them with a lot of crushed garlic and an equal amount of lemon zest. (That is, just the yellow rind of the lemon, with as little as possible of the bitter white pith. I use a peeler, like the peeler you would use for carrots.) Once the olives, garlic, and lemon zest are combined, I cover the whole shooting match with extra-virgin olive oil. Now, you really needn't commit expensive oil to this endeavor. Just choose a good, solid one. Here is a perfect example of why I am so proud of our Fairway-label extra-virgin olive oils. They're head and shoulders above any olive oil you could possibly find at retail for even three times the price. Lots of stores private-label an olive oil, and all of these oils are, in a word, boring. The reason—and I am telling you one of the greatest truths in this book—is that the people responsible for choosing the oil know little about it. They've decided the qualifier "extra-virgin" is all that's important, that their customers will never know the difference or will be indifferent to the joys and nuances of what is one of the most important ingredients in their kitchen. As if any olive oil is olive oil. . . . But enough of this prelude to what I want you to know about olive oil. That's coming up. At the moment, we are dealing with olives.

The third olive I chose to offer at the cheese counter was known as an "oil-cured" olive, which is a misnomer. These intensely flavorful, obsidian-black, wrinkled olives are not cured in oil; they're cured in sea salt. That's why they're wrinkled. The salt draws out considerably more moisture than does brine or a lye solution. Most oil-cured olives are imported from Greece,

PREVIOUS SPREAD:
*Cracked Sicilians at
one of the stores*

THE FOOD LIFE

Niçoise Salad

Serves 4

Niçoise salad is defined by the tuna. It is *not* fresh tuna; it is high-end tuna from a can or jar, packed in olive oil (or brine, but you rarely see high-end brined tuna). Look for these brands: Ortiz, El Batel, Flott, Zoe, As Do Mar.

1. Place the eggs in a large saucepan with water to cover and bring the water to a boil. Simmer for 1 minute, then cover the pan, remove it from the heat, and let it sit for 10 minutes. Drain the eggs and run them under cold water until cool enough to handle. Peel and thinly slice the eggs. Set aside.

2. While the eggs are cooking, boil the potatoes in salted water until fork-tender, 20 to 30 minutes. Drain the potatoes, and once they are cool enough to handle, thinly slice them crosswise. Set aside.

3. In a steamer basket or strainer set over simmering water, steam the haricots verts until just tender, about 10 minutes. Let cool.

4. To serve, divide the mixed greens among 4 plates. Top each with tuna and season with salt and pepper. On each plate, arrange egg slices, potato slices, haricots verts, bell pepper, radishes, cucumbers, and cherry tomatoes. Garnish each plate with a few olives, a few onion slices, and 2 crisscrossed anchovies. Do *not* toss. This salad looks best if the ingredients remain separate and colorful. Drizzle with Dijon vinaigrette.

8 large eggs

12 fingerling or small Red Bliss new potatoes, unpeeled

2 handfuls haricots verts, trimmed (see Chef's Note)

4 handfuls mixed salad greens (about 6 ounces)

12 ounces good-quality tuna packed in olive oil, drained

Kosher or sea salt and freshly ground black pepper, to taste

1 small red bell pepper, cored and cut into thin rounds

8 radishes, scrubbed and thinly sliced

2 Kirby cucumbers, thinly sliced

½ cup cherry or grape tomatoes, halved

¼ cup Niçoise olives (pitted or not—live dangerously)

¼ red onion, peeled and very thinly sliced

8 oil-packed anchovy fillets

¾ cup Dijon Vinaigrette dressing (see recipe, page 193)

Chef's Note: At the risk of repeating myself, in my opinion haricots verts are really good only when they are *fully* cooked—and, traditionally, the French agree. Since the basis of this salad is a classic French *salade Niçoise,* cook your beans.

but this style of olive is found all around the Mediterranean basin. Oil-cured olives have many, many devotees because of their intense olive flavor. It is a wallop, compared with the nutty caress of a ripe taggiasca, the principal olive of the Italian Riviera as well as that of southern France—Provence and the Midi to the west of Provence. The way I found these olives dressed and presented in Provence was the way I wanted to offer them at Fairway. Once again, crushed fresh garlic is primary, but this time the costarring ingredient is bruised branches of fresh rosemary. The branches are whacked with the dull side of a chef's knife in order to release the volatile rosemary oil that so alluringly perfumes the olives. The glorious flavor of these three dressed olives aside, it is also the visual joy of each that makes the whole effort so exciting. The red and green of chile peppers, the creamy beige of garlic, the dusty green of cracked Sicilians, the gold-green of olive oil, the papal yellow of lemon zest and the reddish-purple of Gaetas, the glossy, stark blackness of oil-cured olives against the piney green of rosemary.

Whoa. This cheese counter was standing on its hind legs and barking like a circus dog. How wonderful to be among cheeses of this caliber and olives dressed to kill, not to mention the wild mushrooms and filled pastas, the colors and textures, the funky fragrances and the prospect of getting to taste anything you could point at. What could be more fun? Not a bad way to spend five and six days a week, week in and week out, for the rest of your professional life.

The success of these and other dressed olives soon made selling from bowls unmanageable and obsolete. The bowls were rarely more than half full. I decided the olives had to be sold from thirty-pound tubs approachable from two sides, and that there had to be thirty-six to forty-eight tubs, each filled with a different olive, some with a mix of three or more olives, and many not so specifically dressed. All, though, would be washed and covered with extra-virgin olive oil. I also chose to offer kosher pickles here—half-sour Kirby cucumbers and full-sours of regular cukes—as well as pickled tomatoes, salted and brined capers, guindilla peppers from Aragon in Spain, sun-dried

OPPOSITE:
Olives and other things, dressed and ready to go.

tomatoes with fresh garlic and basil, peppercorns and extra-virgin olive oil, preserved lemons. I also included one of the most singular items I have ever pioneered and imported, Alsatian sauerkraut, or *choucroute d'Alsace;* it is shipped to me in fifty-five-pound plastic tubs, having been aged over a year in Riesling wine with *saindoux,* or fatback, which renders this sublime kraut nonkosher, alas.

Our olive "gardens"—with all their associated delicacies—became a most profitable per-square-foot of real estate in the stores, to the tune of thousands of pounds of olives every week.

Lentils with Garlic Sausage

Serves 4

One of my top ten favorite things to eat is lentils, particularly du Puy lentils from the Auvergne region of France, and Berry lentils from the region just north of there (also where most of my great goat cheeses come from), not to mention the rare pink lentils from the Champagne region.

I love to serve this already savory, hearty French meal with my exemplary *choucroute d'Alsace*. It makes friends with all French sausages.

1. In a large pot, cover the lentils with 2 inches of cold water. Add 1 of the garlic cloves and the thyme and parsley, and bring to a boil. Reduce the heat, cover, and let the lentils cook at a gentle simmer for 15 minutes. At this point these quick-cooking lentils should be almost tender. Stir in ½ teaspoon salt, cover again, and simmer until soft, but not mushy, 3 to 5 minutes more. Drain the lentils, removing and discarding the garlic clove and herb sprigs. Return the lentils to the pot and keep it covered off the heat, so they stay warm.

2. While the lentils are simmering, poach the sausage by putting it in another pan with the remaining garlic clove, the peppercorns, and water to cover. Bring the water to a very low simmer and cook gently, covered, until the sausage is heated through, about 15 minutes. Do not let the water boil, as boiling will toughen the sausage. Drain the sausage and cut it into ½-inch-thick rounds.

3. Return the lentils to low heat and add the vinaigrette, stirring until the lentils are heated through. To serve, mound the lentils on warmed plates and top each portion with sausage slices. Serve with mustard, cornichons, and bread (lots of sweet cream butter on the bread would definitely not hurt).

2 cups du Puy lentils, picked over to remove pebbles and rinsed

2 large garlic cloves, peeled

1 sprig fresh thyme

1 sprig flat-leaf parsley

Kosher or sea salt

¾ pound fully cooked or smoked garlic sausage (a French *saucisson à l'ail* is the classic way to go, but a good alternative is smoked andouille, Portuguese linguica, or even a good kielbasa, casing or rind peeled away)

1 teaspoon whole black peppercorns

¼ cup Grainy Mustard Vinaigrette (see recipe, page 193)

Dijon mustard, cornichons, and crusty sourdough bread, for serving

Grocer's Note: Du Puy lentils are small, thin-skinned dark-green lentils that have actually been granted AOC status in the Auvergne region. (AOC stands for *Appellation d'Origine Contrôlée,* meaning French government–certified name control.) These lentils are less starchy than other varieties, so that they keep their shape and do not turn mushy when cooked.

11

In Praise
of
Olive Oil

My pores ooze olive oil. And that's good, except for the bed linen. For the past decade I have spent more time at tasks related to olive oil than with cheese or anything else. We at Fairway are so consumed by olive oil you would think (wrongly) that we owned and operated a sizable olive grove somewhere. This is the way I was consumed by cheese from 1975 until about 2000, when I began to wean myself off it (well, to some degree). As with cheese, I don't make olive oil. But I've done and continue to do everything else with it. Source it, criticize it, heap scorn on it, laud it, import it, and sell it at retail. Smell it, rub it into my skin in order to smell it, rub it into my hair for the health of my scalp, taste it, cook with it (actually, as I've said, Michelle does the cooking), pour it over more things I regularly enjoy eating than is really necessary (things like steak, hamburgers, fresh sheep's and goat's milk cheeses, boiled shrimp, toast, cottage cheese, and melon). And is there anything more satisfying—anything—than an *aglio ed olio* sauce for pasta featuring not just good olive oil and crushed or minced garlic, but also a couple of chopped fillets of anchovy and a dab of *harissa*?

I like to watch olives grow, climb olive trees (tree-climbing was a favorite activity all my young life), watch olives being harvested, watch olives being crushed, watch nascent olive oil being separated from the olive oil water, watch olive oil being bottled. . . . And I've done these things in most of the countries around the Mediterranean basin, where olive oil comes from. Yes, I know it comes from other places, too. But olive oil is first and foremost a Mediterranean phenomenon.

I have learned that there are about 2,000 varieties of olives, of which perhaps 200 figure in the business of olives and olive oil. My oil inventory represents two dozen or so varieties. Of that number, I *could* make do with about half. But I won't. As with cheese, I am more a curator than a retailer.

The first extra-virgin olive oil I ever dealt with was brought to me by my old friend Leo Shaw, a wine importer and salesman in cahoots with a Tuscan winemaker whose well-known Chianti has one of those lyrical names that shout out their egocentrism. Many, if not all, Tuscan vineyards share real estate with olive groves, and it made sense to them to market their olive oil as they did their wine—in fancy bottles with fancier labels, and with prices as lofty as the market would allow.

So I bought and sold this first super-Tuscan olive oil at the Pasta & Cheese shops on the Upper East Side. It got a lot of attention *(New York Times,* and elsewhere) and sold well, despite its extortionate price. I didn't know anything about olive oil, so the price didn't make any difference to me.

The only competition this Tuscan oil had at that time (1979) was three particular brands of "French" olive oil in pretty bottles—they looked great on the kitchen counter. But they were phony and piss-elegant. First, at least one of them wasn't extra-virgin, and though the other two claimed to be, I suspect they weren't. In those days, you could get away with murder on labels, not just for olive oil, but really for anything. The big story is that not a drop of any of those oils came from olives grown in France. The oil was Greek, Spanish, or Italian. In those days, that meant it was cheap. All you had to do was have it trucked to Wherever, France; give it a phony-baloney name; bottle it; label it; and sell it. And the fancier you made it look, the more you could charge.

It must be said that there were a lot of brands of affordable olive oil back then, but they were sold in the ethnic neighborhoods of New York or elsewhere in America, enclaves of expatriate or first-generation Italians and Greeks. These oils were mostly packed in Italy, but once again not necessarily pressed from olives grown in Italy. They weren't mainstream enough to have been picked up by the supermarket distribution channels. And they weren't good oil. They weren't even extra-virgin.

OK, what does extra-virgin mean? Well, at least two things. First, legally, it means that the olives were "cold-pressed," pressed without the use of an old factory press that employs heat and hot water, as well as great pressure, in order to extract every smudge of grease from the olive mulch. This way of separating oil from an olive is violent and understandably injurious to the oil, which is notoriously delicate and flighty.

STEVE'S BLOG OF THE DAY
May 8, 2006

One of the greatest trips I ever got to take was to Tunisia, where *harissa* (served with couscous) is a sacrament. Tunisians make their own *harissa*, from hot chiles grown at home, strung, garlanded, and festooning nearly every house you pass. To make *harissa*, they're seeded, crushed, and combined into a thick paste with sea salt and any combination of caraway, cumin, coriander, and sometimes mint, garlic, and olive oil. North Africans would never dream of buying commercial *harissa*, but there are several perfectly acceptable examples available here in specialty food shops and even supermarkets. I seem to have a jar or tube of *harissa* on the table constantly in order to bombard my taste buds, to stun myself. I put it on baked potatoes, roasted onions, french fries, beef stew. It's a natural with my wife's staggeringly wonderful minestrone of short ribs, beans, cabbage, onions, carrots, and the rest of their friends ladled over thick *tranches* (slabs) of crusty bread, drizzled with a robust, unfiltered olive oil and dusted with grated Parmigiano.

Harissa is quite welcome at these and other venues, and would be sorely missed.

SUPER-SPECIAL

CRISMONA SPANISH
UN-FILTERED EXTRA-VIRGIN
BAENA (ANDALUCIA) OLIVE OIL

FROM THE HOME OF THE GREAT NUNEZ DE PRADO OLIVE OIL, LIP-SMACKING OF GRANNY SMITH APPLES AND SEVILLE ORANGES, COMES FAIRWAY'S CHALLENGER CRISMONA, FROM JUST DOWN THE LITERAL ROAD. WE DEFY YOU TO TASTE THE DIFFERENCE BETWEEN NUNEZ AND CRISMONA! SO WHAT IS THE DIFF? WELL, NUNEZ RETAILS FOR TWICE THE PRICE OF OUR CRISMONA! HIGHWAY ROBBERY, PURE AND SIMPLE. FAIRWAY IS THE REPOSITORY OF TRUTH IN OLIVE OIL. AND EVERYBODY KNOWS IT.

FAIRWAY
"Like No Other Market"

$5.99
½ LITER
BTL

Second, also legally, extra-virgin means that the oil has a very small, though measurable, percentage of acid. Too much acid can impart a rancid and often bitter flavor and smell, because acidity is a measure of oxidation, or spoilage. If there's a lot, the oil wasn't handled very assiduously, from the harvesting method (bruising) to the length of time taken in pressing the olives after harvest (more than a few hours is olive abuse) to the amount of air, light, and heat the new oil is exposed to.

The enemies of fine olive oil are time, air, light, and heat. As for time, olive oil, unlike some wines and cheeses, does not improve in the bottle or can. If you are a family of four and you're using less than a liter of grand olive oil a week, you need to use more olive oil—but that's another issue. (By "grand" I mean not merely that the oil is extra-virgin, but also that it is remarkable, full of nuance, fragrant—it has a rich mouthfeel without being cloying or greasy.)

In olive oil, the flavor and fragrance molecules run down like flashlight batteries. But I'll bet you that unless you're a regular at Fairway, any bottle or tin of purportedly grand olive oil you pick up either won't tell when the oil was produced or will reveal in very fine print that it's been in that bottle for two years or longer. Absolutely unacceptable.

Air, oxidation, causes oil to become stale, flat, lifeless. Light robs oil of its color, nutrients, flavor, and fragrance. It does this right through the glass, even if the bottle has never been opened. How does it do that? I don't know. It just does.

Heat robs olive oil, indeed any culinary oil, of its organoleptic properties. This is why you should never cook with grand olive oil unless you are a hopeless wastrel. Don't store your olive oil where common sense tells you not to—in a hot pantry, next to the oven or stove, or on a hot windowsill or radiator.

I'd never use the legally designated "pure" olive oil for any reason, other than perhaps as an emollient for my skin (and I don't see that happening). "Pure" is a strictly enforced industry definition for olive oil which has been so refined that it is merely grease—thin, limpid, flavorless, aroma-less, worthless in any serious kitchen or any kitchen that aspires to be serious. It has had chemical solvents added to the original mulch, which, when olives are pressed, is the first step of extracting oil. Then every bit of nonsolid substance is extracted as the mulch is reheated and centrifuged faster than a speeding bullet. It may then be blended with cheaper, more tasteless and colorless "pure" oil. There are a couple of even more shameful and shameless legal purity levels of olive oil beneath "pure" that don't merit discussion. They are used in "food service," the industry that supplies restaurants and institutions with the cheapest possible ingredients. Some big companies blend "pure" olive oil with canola (rapeseed) oil, to bring the price down even lower.

It is not uncommon for crooks in the olive oil business to get caught. They blend olive oil with sunflower oil or refined hazelnut oil, which is tasteless and cheap, and export it as pure olive oil. You might think that's not a big deal, but it is. Not long ago, some disreputable Spanish olive oil producer blended olive oil with a non-food-grade linseed oil, just for domestic consumption, and the oil killed a lot of people. But that hasn't happened since. What about the super-Tuscan olive oil that I mentioned as being the first high-end olive oil in New York? There was a big, bad freeze in Europe in 1987. Uncountable olive trees froze solid and died. There were absolutely no olives harvested in Tuscany that year. But surprise, surprise—come late winter and early spring of 1988, the 1987 pressing of that very super-Tuscan began. I never did business with the producers again, and to this day, when I see a store offering their oil, I consider it a store that knows nothing about olive oil.

Salads: Steakhouse Caesar Salad

Serves 4

It is said, and I believe it, that the Caesar salad was invented in 1924 by Caesar Cardini, who owned a restaurant in Tijuana, Mexico. We have all been served many versions of Caesar salad. They're rarely better than pretty good, and they mostly range from pedestrian all the way down to just a really boring mess. Mitchel's, as you might guess, is definitive, and that's because he never stints on the quality of the ingredients—for Caesar salad or anything else. So use only superb, extra-virgin olive oil and good anchovies. Supermarket-quality anchovies, for instance, will ruin the salad—they're too fishy, too salty.

1. In a large salad bowl, combine the anchovy fillets and garlic. Using two forks and a little elbow grease, mash them together to make a rough paste. Add the egg yolks and mustard and mix thoroughly with a fork. Beat in the lemon juice. Add 1 cup of the croutons and use a fork to crush them into the dressing (this is what gives the dressing its texture—you want to feel the crunch of croutons in each bite). Slowly pour in the olive oil in a steady stream, beating constantly, until the dressing is creamy and emulsified. Season with salt and pepper to taste.

2. Add the romaine and toss well. Sprinkle in the Parmesan and toss again. Toss in the remaining croutons and serve.

6 to 8 anchovy fillets

2 garlic cloves, peeled and put through a press

3 large egg yolks, raw (or coddled, if you insist; see Grocer's Note)

1 to 2 tablespoons Dijon mustard, to taste

3 tablespoons freshly squeezed lemon juice

3 cups Parmesan-Garlic Croutons (see recipe, page 99)

½ cup extra-virgin olive oil

Kosher or sea salt and freshly ground black pepper, to taste

2 hearts of romaine lettuce, torn into bite-size pieces

½ cup coarsely grated Parmesan cheese

Chef's Note: The problem with making a Caesar salad in a restaurant is that everybody has an opinion about what makes a good one, and everybody likes a different proportion of one ingredient or another. (As far as I'm concerned, there's no room in a Caesar salad for Worcestershire sauce or—apologies to my wife—Tabasco.) Therefore, it's the perfect salad to make at home, where you can tailor it to your tastes.

Grocer's Note: If you're concerned about the safety of raw eggs, you can coddle, or lightly cook, them. Gently lower them into boiling water and keep the water at an active simmer for 2 minutes. Drain the eggs and run cool water over them; then use a sharp knife to crack the shells and split the eggs in half, letting the contents spill into a bowl. Pour off and discard the loose egg white; use the coddled yolks in the dressing.

Bagna Cauda

Serves 8

Bagna cauda means "hot bath" in Italian. Typically, a crock of this dipping sauce of olive oil, garlic, and anchovy is placed in the center of the table over a heating element to keep it warm. With a nice spread of crisp veggies, it's better for your soul than chips and dip.

CRUDITÉS:

½ bunch asparagus, trimmed

¼ pound haricots verts, trimmed

1 head endive, leaves separated

½ bunch broccoli, large florets only

¼ head cauliflower, broken into small yet dippable florets

1 fennel bulb, cored and sliced

1 bunch radishes, scrubbed and trimmed

1 seedless hothouse cucumber (or a few small Kirby cukes), cut into spears

1 pint cherry or grape tomatoes

BAGNA CAUDA:

2 cups extra-virgin olive oil

10 to 12 oil-packed anchovy fillets

3 garlic cloves, peeled and sliced as thinly as possible (a mandoline is useful here)

Freshly ground black pepper

1. Blanch the asparagus spears in boiling salted water for 2 minutes, then plunge them into an ice bath to stop them from cooking. Drain them and pat them dry. Boil the haricots verts until crisp-tender, plunge them into an ice bath, drain them, and pat them dry.

2. Assemble the crudités on a platter around a small bowl, which will hold the bagna cauda.

3. In a small saucepan over very low heat, warm the olive oil, anchovies, and garlic. Stir gently with a wooden spoon to break up the anchovy fillets; as the mixture gets hotter, the anchovies should start to liquefy. The whole process should take no more than 5 minutes (you do not want the garlic to brown). Season the bagna cauda with black pepper to taste (it should already be salty enough, thanks to the anchovies), pour it into the bowl, and serve.

Chef's Note: The traditional way to serve bagna cauda is like a miniature fondue, in a heat-proof pot in a stand over a small flame. If you plan to serve it as part of a buffet, this is a good idea.

I keep learning new things about olive oil. Here's a news flash. The prevailing wisdom and confident opinion among four technical experts (technical as well as aesthetic) on olive oil—a Spaniard, an Italian, and two Frenchmen—is that the sought-after, highly touted low acidity (less than 1 percent) known as "extra-virgin-ness" is no measure of quality. They say extra-virgin olive oil must oxidize, be acidic, to some degree in order for several of its organoleptic properties—the properties that make olive oil smell and taste as it does—to come to the fore. Now, that's a hot one. I'm buying it, and it goes against everything that other "experts" have been hammering us with for years. So here's what to do: *Ignore a label proclaiming "less than 1 percent acidity" and concentrate instead on where and who the oil came from, and when. Where* first, because unless you have a grasp of regions, you really have no grasp whatsoever of what you like. There is absolutely no point in referring to an oil—or any foodstuff, for that matter—as French, Spanish, or whatever. There is no unity, nor are there any identifying or telltale characteristics, to define an olive oil as being from a given country. When a shopper at Fairway comes up to me and says, "I want a Spanish oil," it is clear that I'm going to have to be gentle, because this person knows nothing about the subject. The grand olive oils of Spain are as different from each other as wines, cheeses, and people. All these things look the same, but they sure don't taste the same. Now, if the shopper had said, "I want a Catalan oil" or "I want a Provençal oil," well, let's have a little chat.

A few years ago, some olive oil producers jumped aboard the despicable "lite" bandwagon and started making a lot of money by proclaiming that the reduced fat in their product offers a great dietary benefit. This is patently absurd. Everything they took away was exactly what makes olive oil so good for you. I hesitate to go into the health benefits of olive oil, because although I have studied it in depth, and I truly believe olive oil is a miracle food, health stuff bores the bejesus out of me, and besides, it has already been written about ad nauseam.

Ligurian Potatoes

Serves 4

This is a sophisticated take on potato salad, using the veggies from a traditional Ligurian pesto. It also provides a fitting opportunity to use one of the marvelous olive oils from Liguria, the Italian Riviera, which extends from the French border at Ventimiglia all the way up and around Genoa and down past Rapallo and the achingly gorgeous Cinque Terre to the border of Tuscany at Carrara. The olive oil from this part of the world is gentle and delicately though unmistakably fragrant.

1. In a small dry skillet over medium heat, toast the pine nuts, tossing occasionally, until lightly golden, about 2 minutes. Transfer them to a plate to stop the cooking.

2. Boil the haricots verts in salted water until fully cooked and tender, about 8 minutes. Drain well and let cool.

3. Boil the potatoes in salted water until fully cooked and tender, about 30 minutes. Drain them and transfer them to a large serving bowl. Add the crushed garlic and the olive oil while the potatoes are still hot. Mix well with a fork, breaking the potatoes into large chunks. Let sit for 10 to 15 minutes.

4. Add the cooked beans, basil, and toasted pine nuts. Season with salt and freshly ground black pepper and toss gently, taking care not to break up the potatoes too much more. If you must have some color, since I made you cook the bright green out of the green beans, toss in some halved cherry tomatoes just before serving.

¼ cup pine nuts

½ teaspoon kosher or sea salt, plus additional to taste

6 ounces haricots verts, trimmed

1 pound new potatoes (any small, thin-skinned variety), unpeeled

2 garlic cloves, peeled and put through a press or finely crushed

¼ cup extra-virgin olive oil

½ cup fresh basil leaves, roughly chopped

Freshly ground black pepper to taste

½ cup cherry tomatoes, halved (optional)

Chef's Note: Remember that all nuts will continue to darken for a few minutes after you remove them from the heat, so don't take your eyes off them while they are toasting and pull them off the stove before they reach the color you really want.

Our beloved Fairway-label extra-virgin olive oils are cheaper than the same quantity of those national brand idiotic "pure" or even "lite" olive oils. This means they're cheap enough to sauté with or to fry with, even though they are far too good to be used that way. So many people overpay for a grand olive oil and then know enough not to cook with it but are not informed enough to know that the "pure" olive oil they buy for cooking doesn't deserve to be taken seriously. It will smoke, it will burn, and it will flavor your food accordingly. Stock your kitchen with strictly extra-virgin olive oil, but try to find one that isn't so expensive that you wouldn't cook with it. Keep the grand oils around for vinaigrettes, for drizzling and dribbling, for marinating, for basting, and to use as ready-made sauce at the table.

OPPOSITE:
The store at Broadway and 74th Street; note the "barrel" oils at left-center.

You must have a loud olive oil, one with the initial, slight, incipient bitterness so characteristic of early-harvest oils; this oil must have layers of flavor and a peppery finish. I refer to such oils as robust, and they come from lots of places, lots of groves, and lots of olive varieties. Don't be too focused on olive varieties if you're just getting started. Their pretty names and their particular characteristics will come.

You must also have in the kitchen at all times a quiet olive oil. Fragrant and sweet, grassy and herby, with sometimes a suggestion of citrus or green tomato. The finest gentle oils come from a lot of places, too, and from several varieties of olives. So I want you to have at least three olive oils in your kitchen at all times. This doesn't address the nut oils, seed oils, and the like that bring such value to your food life. We'll get to them.

Your gentle oil and your loud oil should not necessarily be pigeonholed, as is the common practice, so that you assign the loud oil to robust dishes and, accordingly, the gentle oil to delicate dishes. Rather, you should follow your own subjective inclinations. Maybe you like the flavor of the robust oil with grilled fish, instead of a gentle oil that might seem to complement the mild flavors better. Maybe you like the way the gentle oil doesn't add any heaviness to a fine winter minestrone laden with cabbage and short ribs, beans and aromatic vegetables.

Until a few years ago, Fairway's selection of olive oils was made up of our house label, a marvelous blend of Umbrian and Pugliese (Umbria and Puglia are two Italian regions you must study) extra-virgins, and every grand oil I could get my hands on. Several of these imports, oils brought in by local and not-so-local distributors, have been with us for decades. But I had become increasingly annoyed at having to buy oil selected by someone else. So I decided that our array would be distinguished by oils imported exclusively by us. I had done a lot of traveling, and I already knew what grand oils were out there waiting for me. But I began to visit mills again in earnest, to find the very best oils in existence, not just those available from local suppliers. I started with rare Provençal French oils from groves that have been local heroes for many, many years, but that had never been picked up by North American importers. I now import twenty labels, some name-controlled as to their provenance and olive type. Some are from Provence, and there are several from various regions in Italy and Spain. They are all absolutely thrilling.

But that's not the half of it. I wanted to private-label some of the world's finest olive oils. I now bring in barrels of unfiltered, extra-virgin, name-controlled olive oils from eleven far-flung groves in the Mediterranean basin, Australia, and California, so that we can hand-pump these elegant, super-fresh oils into bottles ourselves. I wanted to offer these stunningly delicious oils in unfancy bottles with labels I myself designed and wrote. Well, I didn't design them. Fairway's graphics genius, Armando Gonzalez, did. But I wrote the labels, and that's my point. I wanted to have labels that told the reader as much as possible about each oil, where it came from, when it was harvested and pressed, what it smells like, what it tastes like, how I like to use it, and how to take care of it.

After the oils themselves, what I love most about this project is not only that we can lay claim to these great sources, but that we can offer the oil at prices as low as they can possibly be, owing to the bulk oil price, my relationship with the producers of the oils, and our huge and frequent orders. Plus, as the importer, I have cut out the importer's profit, as well as the broker's and the distributor's. I figure out exactly what the oil cost to put on the stand and then take the usual Fairway markup, which has always been the real reason Fairway is such a powerhouse—our prices are always lower than our competitors'. The rich get richer for a reason: they're usually doing a better job than everybody else.

As I've said, other oils can add value to your food life, too: namely nut, seed, and kernel oils. The first time I tasted walnut oil was in 1979. As I recall, I was having lunch with Giorgio DeLuca at Beauvilliers, a highly regarded restaurant in Paris near Montmartre. We were served a wonderful salad of mâche, also a first for me. Mâche is a salad green cherished by French food lovers; its English name is lambs' tongues, lambs' lettuce, or field salad. This salad also contained thinly sliced shallot and slivers of grapefruit, but what made it especially memorable was its vinaigrette, which was made with sherry wine vinegar—yet another first for me—and walnut oil. (Try that sometime when you're making vinaigrette. It has become a house staple for Michelle and me.) At that time, I don't believe any store in New York sold walnut oil. Giorgio and I swore an oath at that restaurant that Dean & DeLuca would never be out of it, and the store never was.

Walnut oil is delicious but somewhat obtrusive and heavy, so don't hesitate to dilute it a bit with olive oil or a more neutral oil such as sunflower, safflower, or grapeseed. Another great nut oil, hazelnut oil, is lighter. It, too, is delicious and fragrant, lends itself amicably to salad dressings, and serves as a table condiment to anoint this or that cooked meat, seafood, or vegetable. Beware cheap hazelnut oil, though. You want a high-quality, cold-pressed, unrefined French oil. You'll recognize the difference. Undistinguished hazelnut oil is much cheaper than olive oil; therefore, a processor who can get away with it stands to make a lot of money. Low-quality hazelnut oil has also been known to be surreptitiously blended with olive oil by shady olive oil processors. Look for our Lapalisse brand.

Spaghetti with Gratinéed Zucchini and Chopped Pignoli

Serves 4

This recipe is heavenly. My wife, Michelle, makes it for us frequently. Mitchel says he loves to take a tub of it with him when he has to travel by air.

½ cup pignoli nuts (see Grocer's Note)

6 medium zucchini, sliced into ¼-inch rounds (see Chef's Note)

7 tablespoons extra-virgin olive oil

1 cup grated Parmesan cheese, plus additional for serving, if desired

½ to 1 tablespoon red pepper flakes, to taste

Kosher or sea salt

1 pound dry spaghetti

Freshly ground black pepper, to taste

1. Preheat the oven to 475°F. In a medium, dry skillet over medium heat, toast the pine nuts until golden brown, about 3 minutes. Transfer them to a plate to cool, then chop them roughly and set them aside.

2. Spread the zucchini rounds evenly on 2 rimmed sheet pans. Drizzle each pan with 2½ tablespoons of the olive oil, then sprinkle each pan with half of the Parmesan and the red pepper flakes. Roast the zucchini, rotating the pans front to back and top to bottom halfway through, until the zucchini is tender and browned, 20 to 25 minutes.

3. While the zucchini roasts, bring a large pot of salted water to a boil. Cook the spaghetti until it is al dente. Drain well and transfer it to a large, warmed serving bowl. Add the zucchini and chopped pignoli, drizzle with the remaining 2 tablespoons olive oil, and season with salt and pepper. Toss and top with more grated Parmesan, if desired, before serving.

Chef's Note: No need for a mandoline to slice the zucchini. It is fine if the slices aren't all the same thickness. That adds a nice texture to the dish: some slices will be soft while others have a little more crunch.

Grocer's Note: Pine nuts (aka pignoli), of the genus *Pinus,* grow in the northern hemisphere. They are among the most expensive nuts in the world, but not because the trees are rare—there are about 20 trillion pine trees in the world. These nuts are expensive because they're such a pain in the butt to get out of the cone. Pine nuts are shelled by hand. There ain't no machine. Hand labor = high price. (The same goes for black walnuts, the world's most delicious nut.)

An inferior variety of pine nut, *Pinus koraiensis* from Korea, is often sold at wholesale and retail. You should know that the best pine nuts are slender and pointy, whereas the others are bigger and fatter. If what you're looking at is confusing, you can be sure they are *not* real pine nuts if the retail price is less than $15 per pound. The Korean nuts are not bad; they're just not the same.

Pine nuts get stale faster than other nuts, so you also want a shop where the turnover is brisk and where you trust your retailer. Pine nuts can get rancid, too, because of their amazing amount of fragile oil. Pine nut oil, by the way, is delicious as a table condiment, but it, too, is very expensive, not to mention hard to find, unless you shop at a Fairway.

The Smoke Point of Oils for Cooking

The smoke point indicates how much heat an oil can take before actually beginning to smoke. Smoking releases carcinogens into the air and free radicals within the oil—and tastes bad—so choose the right oil for your project. If you do accidentally heat an oil beyond its smoke point, discard it and start over. The oils below are grouped according to their best uses. They are listed roughly in order of highest smoke point to lowest—but keep in mind that the particular method by which an oil is processed greatly affects its smoke point.

All-Purpose Cooking

Oils with a high smoke point (520°F–440°F) are ideal for sautéing, frying, and other high-heat applications.

Avocado	Apricot kernel
Safflower, superhigh heat	Palm fruit
Almond	Sesame, refined

Baking and Moderate-Heat Sautéing

Oils with a medium-high smoke point (440°F–360°F) are good for sautéing at medium-high heat or, because of their neutral flavor, for baking.

Safflower, unrefined	Walnut, semirefined
Canola or rapeseed	Coconut, unrefined
Grapeseed	Soy, semirefined
Almond	

Light Sautéing and Sauces

These oils have a smoke point between 360°F and 280°F. They normally have fuller flavors, making them ideal for sauces and salad dressing, or for brief sautéing at medium heat when the oil's flavor is intended to be an integral part of the finished dish.

Sesame, cold-pressed, toasted or untoasted	Olive, cold-pressed
Peanut, cold-pressed	Corn, unrefined

I found a roasted (*grillée*) almond oil recently. Almond oil from raw nuts is used in pastry baking and is, oddly, rather neutral-tasting. But this roasted almond oil, cold-pressed by the oldest mill in France, Lapalisse, at the village of that name in the Bourbonnais region, is a revelation. It is so delicious that I recommend it be used as a table condiment, a sort of ready-made sauce for cooked meats and seafood as well as vegetables. Also marvelous as table condiments are the terrific apricot kernel oil and Agen prune pit oil that I import from France. The apricot kernel oil smells like, well, apricots, but with a nutty and vanilla-like nuance. The prune pit oil has a billowing aroma of almonds.

I get grapeseed oil from a fellow north of Nîmes (France) who specializes in it. The bottles wear a Fairway label explaining that this oil is quite neutral in flavor, but despite that fact about grapeseed oil, it is also very fresh-tasting, with a nice aroma. Now, I confess that "fresh-tasting" and "nice aroma" tell you absolutely nothing, but there's just no other way to articulate the qualities of grapeseed oil without being vague or arch, or evasive. I promise: grapeseed oil exudes a freshness that is ineffable, to use another annoying descriptor. It is desirable for those who want a neutral salad oil for whatever reason, but its truest virtue is that it has a high smoke point, making it a perfect cooking oil.

Styrian pumpkinseed oil from Austria is a remarkable table condiment. It has a powerful fragrance of pumpkins that is delightful with many things—for example, seafood, roast chicken, salad greens, and starchy foods like potatoes, rice, and couscous. It is not to be cooked with, though, because it becomes harsh and smokes. The Styrian oil is raw and cold-pressed, and it's a marvel. I have tried domestic pumpkinseed oil, as well as a few versions from other parts of Europe, but they are underwhelming.

Avocado oil is gaining in popularity, although it was unheard of only a couple of years ago. Thick, rich, buttery, and as golden as can be, it's a terrific salad oil.

In addition to sesame oil and toasted sesame oil, peanut oil, and mustardseed oil, you will be likely to come across pistachio oil and pine nut oil, each of which is unique and, while costly, a lot of fun to experiment with.

Notice that I am talking about oils pressed from nuts, seeds, and kernels, not flavored olive oils. I am increasingly irritated by the marketing of olive oil with stuff in it. I suspect that all the stuff with stuff in it—cheeses, breads, infused oils, dipping oils, olive oils blended with vinegar—is an attempt to disguise the fact that the product isn't good enough to stand on its own. A few years ago, my people in California offered me an extra-virgin oil that they had pressed with lemons added right along with the olives—a lemon-infused olive oil. They also had oils that were lime-infused, orange-infused, or garlic-infused. I thought that sounded pretty keen. I must have been getting senile, because it eventually dawned on me that I had fallen for a gimmick. For heaven's sake, if you want a lemon-flavored oil for whatever reason, pull out a lemon and squeeze the juice into the oil. Olio santo *is* legit, though, to my mind. It's a lusty, versatile table condiment that you create the way you make any recipe. I simply have no patience with shortcuts: boutique bread dipping oils with fancy pourers attached to the necks of the bottles, bruschetta toppings in jars. They annoy me to death. White truffle oil? Yuck.

The Fairway-Brand Barrel-Imported Olive Oils

AOC Vallée des Baux-de-Provence
Extra-Virgin French Olive Oil
Unfiltered for Maximum Flavor
The seventeenth-century mill (Moulin Jean-Marie Cornille) is still equipped with the ancient granite grinding stone and the *scourtins* (woven mats) used to cold-press the mulched olives; the resulting oil from a blend of Salonenque, Grossane, Beruguette, Verdale, and Picholine olives is highly fragrant (ripe fruit, black olives, olive paste), powerful, and very complex (a touch of cocoa and, surprisingly, long-aged rum). A remarkable oil, enormous on the palate, suitable as a ready-made sauce for all foods, whether cooked or raw. The groves and mill are just east of Arles in Provence-Alpes-Côte d'Azur (Bouches-du-Rhône).

Australian Picual
Extra-Virgin Olive Oil
This extraordinary oil is grown, harvested, and pressed on the Boort estate in Victoria, north of Melbourne. It is 100 percent Picual, a sweet-style oil with well-balanced bitterness and pepper and tomato flavors dominating the fragrance. It is far too good to cook with. Use it as an anointing oil for seafood and for vegetables, as a dip for bread, for bruschetta and fettunta, as a baste, for marinades, and for vinaigrettes.

Baena DO
Extra-Virgin Olive Oil
Unfiltered for Maximum Flavor
Very fragrant; classic, floral, piney, fresh-cut herbs, fresh-cut wood, crushed leaves; on the palate, sweet, with a touch of bitterness, citrus fruits; surprising strength to the finesse of this remarkable unfiltered oil; a blend of native Picudo, plus Hojiblanca and Picual; of 45,000 hectares (a hectare is about 2.5 acres) yielding 31,000 tons annually, only 6,000 tons of extra-virgin Baena are designated *denominación de origen* (DO). Baena is a subregion of north-central Andalusia (in Spanish, Andalucía), a land of undulating, arid pastures between Córdoba and Castro del Río. We consider this oil, if not the most delicious we have ever tasted, certainly among the top three.

Barbera Sicilian
Extra-Virgin First Cold Pressing
Unfiltered for Maximum Flavor
This unfiltered oil from western Sicily is cold-pressed from Biancolilla olives. It is wonderfully fragrant with an unctuous, creamy texture. Its flavor is immense, complex—dried fruit, hazelnut, black peppercorns. It is provided exclusively for Fairway by Manfredi Barbera, whose Frantoio, Stupor Mundi, and Barbera organic labels are among our most famous and popular olive oils. These olives were harvested in February 2007. The oil's acidity measured less than 0.5 percent. It is recommended for all purposes—salads, vinaigrettes, sauces, bastes, marinades, sautés, dipping, drizzling, anointing.

California
Extra-Virgin Olive Oil
This is our private blend of Mission, Manzanilla, and Sevillano olives, grown, harvested, and pressed (within twenty-four hours of the November harvest) in northern California's Tehama and Butte counties. We taste sweet butter and green apples. It has an obviously fruity fragrance. This is oil too good to cook with. It should be used for vinaigrettes, for marinades, as a baste, and as a ready-made sauce for anointing steaks, seafood, bread, vegetables, and pasta. It has a huge following here, and rightly so. The new vainglorious California olive oils selling at four times the price of this oil can't hold a candle to it.

Catalan Arbequina
Extra-Virgin First Cold Pressing
Unfiltered for Maximum Flavor

The Arbequina olive, tiny and green and purple, grows in Catalonia. The oil pressed from it is justly famous for its light texture and delicious flavor—nutty and fruity, with aromas of almond, cassis, apple, and new-mown hay. Its color ranges from golden to gold-green. This is one of the greatest olive oils, considered suave and sophisticated, sweet and gentle, perfect for all purposes. It should be used within one year of purchase.

DOP Gata-Hurdes
Extra-Virgin Olive Oil
Unfiltered for Maximum Flavor

This is a name-controlled cult olive oil hoarded by Spain's fanatics. It has never before been imported to the United States. Gata-Hurdes is the northernmost subregion of Extremadura, an area of "accidental relief"—gentle sun, abundant rain, and balmy temperatures. The terraced groves are tended to and harvested completely by hand. The sole olive, unique to the valley of the Jerte, and having adapted specifically to the un-olive-like climate, is the manzanilla cacereña. And as with the famous Extremaduran sheep that give so little milk, resulting in the greatest of all cheeses (Torta del Casar and Queso de la Serena), fully twenty-two kilos of the manzanilla cacereña olives are pressed in order to yield one liter of oil. We detect fragrances and flavors of preserved lemon, almond, and green tomato. Decidedly rich and unctuous, this is an oil of enormous personality.

French AOC Nyons
Extra-Virgin French Olive Oil
Unfiltered for Maximum Flavor

The Autrand-Dozol mill at Nyons on the southern edge of the Drôme department was built in 1730 next to the ancient Roman bridge over the Ouveze River. An unctuous, buttery oil that is much more expressive than the lighter oils from farther south, Nyons oil, pressed from the native Tanche olives, has become a virtual cult among French devotees. Its huge aroma offers the perfume of lush green vegetation, ripe fruit, and hints of cocoa; slightly sweet with a touch of the bitterness of almond skin, this oil must be described as elegant and harmonious, with a long and spicy finish, an oil perfect for fish and seafood, salads, vegetables, and "dipping."

Pugliese
Extra-Virgin Olive Oil
Unfiltered for Maximum Flavor

From groves near Martina Franca in the north-central portion of Italy's Puglia region. Pressed from the December harvest of Cortina, Nostrane, Ogliarole, Peranzana, and Rotondella olives, this cloudy oil is enormously grassy, artichoke-like, and vegetal, both in flavor and in fragrance, and has a bit of pepperiness to its finish. You may also detect hints of green tomato and even the slightest touch of mint. We choose not to cook with any oil at this price. We use our Pugliese oil to bring out the flavors of seafood, steaks, soups, and pasta; as a dip for bread and crudités; as a baste; and for marinating.

Trevi-Umbria
Extra-Virgin Olive Oil

At once rich and unctuous, a veritable explosion of fragrances. You could pay four times the price for a Tuscan oil that will not be as good as this Trevi oil, pressed from Frantoio, Leccino, and Maraiolo olives harvested in November and December. This oil is far too good to cook with; use it instead as a ready-made sauce to anoint any foodstuff that would benefit from it. We particularly treasure it for its hints of stone fruit and bitter almond. Finish is peppery.

12

Vinegar: The **Really** Good Stuff

The business of Fairway was pretty much built on salad ingredients. Yes, fruit and cheese and all those other delicacies and extraordinary foods are important, but, my lord, all that lettuce and stuff. For this reason, it has always seemed prudent to make sure Fairway is fanatically committed to olive oil and vinegar—cardinal ingredients, to my mind. It makes sense to me that we wanted Fairway to be Olive Oil and Vinegar Central, and that's certainly what has happened. And just as I'm thrilled by olive oil, I am thrilled—to a lesser degree, though I'd say no less ardently—by vinegar.

Many things gall me about American supermarkets and about the way most Americans eat, but nothing gets to me more than the aisle with all those bottled salad dressings. It distresses me that so many people across America know so little about oils and vinegars and make such bad choices when shopping for them. Well, not *bad* choices—but uninformed, pedestrian choices. That doesn't have to be, once you understand how important oils and vinegars are and how much joy you experience when you take advantage of the really good stuff. We've already discussed oils. After the oil, it's the vinegar that will have the strongest impact on a vinaigrette. There are so many wonderful choices.

Vinegar is made by allowing an alcoholic liquid to ferment. Fermentation is a chemical process by which the alcohol combines with oxygen to produce acetic acid. The original alcoholic liquid might be wine, beer, cider, or even grain alcohol (which is used to make the white vinegar you can buy in gallon jugs and use to make pickles, clear clogged drains, or wash your windows). Wine was probably used for the first vinegars—the word "vinegar" comes from the French *vin aigre,* "sour wine." Vinegar is always sour—because of its acetic acid content—but it also retains many of the distinguishing flavors of the substance from which it came. At Fairway we carry dozens of types of vinegar in hundreds of variations. The superstar is balsamic vinegar.

Giorgio DeLuca, of Dean & DeLuca, pioneered balsamic vinegar in 1978, and I was his right-hand man at the time. Balsamic vinegar dates back to the eleventh century and is historically attributed to Emilia-Romagna, the region of Italy whose capital is Bologna; but its birthplace is the area around Modena, not Bologna. It was originally quaffed straight as a digestif. Balsamic vinegar was thought to be a panacea, and there is some merit to that belief. There are amazing stories and legends about the magic of balsamic vinegar. One is that during the black death of the fourteenth century— bubonic plague—the only survivors of one city on the Italian peninsula (this was before there was an official Italy) were five thieves who had holed up in the dungeon of a castle to wait it out. They survived by drinking the balsamic vinegar stored there.

Balsamic vinegar is different from other culinary vinegars in that it was never wine. It is cooked-down, fermented, acetified juice derived from a re- pressing of the detritus left after grapes have been pressed for wine, mostly

Two Classic Vinaigrettes

Each makes about ¼ cup

I have a big poster hanging over the olive oil areas in our stores that reads, TO USE BOTTLED SALAD DRESSINGS IS TO MISS THE POINT OF SALAD ALTOGETHER. As a statement, that's self-explanatory. The way to a better dressing is simple, too, as these classics prove.

Dijon Vinaigrette

In a medium bowl, combine the mustard with a pinch of salt and some freshly ground black pepper. Whisk in the vinegar. Whisking constantly, drizzle in the olive oil in a very slow trickle until the mixture has emulsified and is an opaque light gold. Use immediately or whisk again as needed. The dressing will keep in a jar at room temperature for 1 week, longer if refrigerated (though the oil will congeal when chilled—let it return to room temperature before using).

- 1 teaspoon Dijon mustard
- Kosher or sea salt and freshly ground black pepper, to taste
- 1 tablespoon red wine vinegar
- 3 tablespoons extra-virgin olive oil

Grainy Mustard Vinaigrette

In a medium bowl, use a fork to combine the mustard and garlic with a pinch of salt and some freshly ground black pepper to form a coarse paste. Whisk in the vinegar. Whisking constantly, drizzle in the olive oil in a very slow trickle until the mixture has emulsified and is an opaque light gold flecked with brown mustard grains. Use immediately or whisk again as needed. The dressing will keep in a jar at room temperature for 3 days (though the oil will congeal when chilled—let it return to room temperature before using).

- 1 teaspoon grainy mustard
- 1 small garlic clove, peeled and minced or put through a garlic press
- Kosher or sea salt and freshly ground black pepper, to taste
- 1 tablespoon red wine vinegar
- 3 tablespoons extra-virgin olive oil

Chef's Note: When a dressing is properly emulsified, it turns creamy and opaque—the oil particles are suspended throughout the vinegar. Mustard helps this process along immeasurably, as does whisking in the oil gradually. Another way to go is simply to combine all the ingredients in a jar, cover it, and shake vigorously. This is the old-school method for using up the very last bit of mustard in a jar! If you do make a dressing that stubbornly stays separated, don't worry; just mix it thoroughly immediately before pouring it over the salad and tossing—it'll still be delicious.

the Lambrusco of Emilia-Romagna. The liquid was aged in a prescribed series of barrels, each made of a different wood—beech, cherry, chestnut, walnut, and so on. The esters of the different wooden barrels proved to have a profound effect on the flavor of the vinegar, which over time intensified and became increasingly complex.

Eventually, balsamic vinegar left the realm of the apothecary and was taken into the kitchen, where it became a sweetener and intensifier in recipes involving meats, poultry, and vegetables. Today, Italians use it in much the same ways, but in America, since 1978, it has become a staple as a salad vinegar. No self-respecting Italian would ever use balsamic vinegar in a vinaigrette. To an Italian, balsamic vinegar is meant for soups and stews, for roasts, as an aperitif, and as a condiment to drizzle over strawberries. Balsamic vinegar very slightly thickens with age. At fifty years, at a hundred years, and even older (and consequently more expensive), balsamic vinegar shouldn't drizzle. It should only dribble.

At Fairway, we have many brands and ages of balsamic vinegar. What I find remarkable is that balsamic vinegar has become such a superstar, and rightfully so in my opinion, that it has been knocked off all over the map. Chileans, Andalusians, Californians, Brits, and even the high-and-mighty French produce versions of Modenese balsamic vinegar. Why would the French copy an Italian foodstuff? The only precedent I can muster is that in 1950 the French "invented" a "new" cheese—Bleu de Bresse—in order to compete against the Lombardy cheese Gorgonzola. And now the French (Chef Joel Robuchon chiefly among them) have even validated a Spanish foodstuff, *jamón ibérico,* the world's greatest pork product. As for French balsamic vinegar, the DeLouis vinegar makers of Limoges have marketed their exquisite apple cider "balsamic" vinegar, Bouquet de Pomme, a well-known brand. The stuff is delicious.

Saba, or *mosto cotto* (cooked must), is similar to balsamic vinegar in that it is made from the pressed skins and seeds of wine grapes and was never wine. It, too, is cooked down until it is sweet and dark, and of an almost thick consistency—but *saba* isn't vinegar, because it isn't allowed to acetify. *Saba* originally came from Le Marche in Italy, and later from Abruzzo and Emilia-Romagna. In the Middle Ages sugar was so costly that ordinary people couldn't afford it. *Saba* was used in its place to sweeten baked goods, and soon it was added to other dishes that required a bit of sweet complexity: certain soups and sauces, as well as braised meats and poultry. Fairway pioneered the importing of *saba* in the late 1990s. It is an excellent choice as a pan deglazer (sauce) for pork, poultry, fish, scallops, calves' liver, and certainly foie gras.

We also import and stock another relative of vinegar, verjus, from Périgord. Verjus is a sprightly liquid derived from squeezing underripe green wine grapes (*verjus* means "green juice"), but not fermenting the mixture. It can be used in place of lemon juice or vinegar in cooking and will brighten the flavor of soups, stews, and sauces.

Banyuls is a wonderful town on the Roussillon coast of France, once part of Catalonia to the south. I could spend a few lifetimes in the area. Every time I visit there, I think about talking Michelle into letting us buy a place. The Catalan side is only a few miles away and is even more beautiful. Salvador Dalí lived nearby, as did Pablo Picasso. The vineyards around Banyuls have long been famous as the source of a sweet red wine of the same name. Banyuls vinegar, too, is sweet, and has found great favor with those of us who love a sweet vinegar in a vinaigrette. It, too, is a grand choice as a pan deglazer.

Makers of wine vinegar are principally French, Spanish, and Italian. Most, but not all, are big companies that produce oceans of industrial-quality vinegar, made from wine that was doubtless well-nigh undrinkable. The result is profitable, to be sure, but the truth is that the vinegar is no better than the wine it came from. I found an artisanal maker of wine vinegar in Charente-Maritime, the part of Bordeaux above the Gironde. M. Agnes selects specific *cépages* (grape varieties) from high-quality winemakers and ages his vinegars for years in oak barrels. Cabernet sauvignon, merlot, sauvignon, and semillon blanc are the grapes he uses, and his cider vinegar from Limousin apple cider is a revelation. He also infuses and ages some of his vinegars with raspberries, tarragon, cinnamon, and clove. One taste of one of his wine vinegars and it becomes immediately apparent how different a serious wine vinegar is from an industrial product.

Sherry wine vinegar is also a passion of ours. As sherry tastes different, so does sherry wine vinegar. Ours is regarded by many experts as the best sherry money can buy. It was the first vinegar produced from the Pedro Ximénez grape; the result is sweet, like balsamic vinegar, but with that sherry flavor, a vinegar crying out for some of the swooning attention that until now has been lavished only on balsamic vinegar. No serious kitchen should be without Lustau sherry wine vinegar. Sherry, of course, is a British corruption of the name of its origin, Jerez de la Frontera, south of Seville. I highly recommend a visit to Jerez and its purlieus: the national park Coto Doñana, the white towns, and certainly Seville itself, within an easy drive.

Finally, anything, certainly any foodstuff that can prove it was made in Catalonia is something a food lover should take seriously. Catalan food is a marvel—simple, lusty, timeless. The region produces superb wines, and as you might guess, superb wine vinegars. Fairway stocks Catalan vinegars that are unique to the category. I refer to Catalan vinegar made from the muscatel grape, another alluringly sweet vinegar, as is the remarkable vermouth vinegar. Vermouth has long been held in great favor by Catalans. Catalan cava, the beloved sparkling white wine from the area, also makes splendid wine vinegar.

Grilled Marinated Sliced Steak

Serves 4

Mitchel is huge on flank steak; not just because it's always inexpensive, but also because he insists that the flavor is very good, very intense. Plan ahead for this dish, since the meat spends a day in the fridge.

1. Combine the vinegar and oil in a flat-bottom casserole dish or bowl big enough to hold the steak. Rub the steak with the garlic cloves, salt, and pepper. Put the seasoned steak in the oil-and-vinegar mixture, turning it to coat all sides. Drop in the garlic cloves, cover, and marinate in the refrigerator for 24 hours.
2. To cook the steak, preheat a grill or broiler. Grill the steak for 3 minutes on each side or transfer it to a broiler pan and broil it for 4 minutes on each side for medium-rare (this cut is best eaten medium-rare). Place the meat on a cutting board and let it rest for 5 minutes. Slice the meat thinly against the grain and serve.

- 2 tablespoons red wine vinegar
- 1 tablespoon extra-virgin olive oil
- 1 flank steak (about 1½ pounds)
- 2 garlic cloves, peeled and smashed
- ½ teaspoon kosher or sea salt, plus additional to taste
- ½ teaspoon freshly ground black pepper

Chef's Note: My Italian wife likes to add a few sprigs of fresh rosemary to the marinade. Drop the sprigs in when you add the crushed garlic cloves.

13

Adventures in Importing—

Highs and Lows

Sometime in 2000, I began importing foodstuffs direct from Europe. I had been importing all our French cheeses direct since 1996, but until then it never crossed my mind that I had the means to bring in nearly anything I wanted. All I had to do was source it out—that is, find somebody to make it for us. My idea of the best time anyone could possibly have was to drive all over France, Italy, and Spain, as well as the other countries in Europe, shopping at every market and farm stand to see what was out there, what was on the shelves and in the kitchens of any particular region. It became apparent that what was available to us in New York was exasperatingly limited to the whims and fancies of "specialty food" importers and to growers of produce in California. And if it was on our shelves, it was doubtless on the shelves of every other store too. Nothing special about that.

One of the very first things I came across that I knew would be a big hit was beets. Lots of New Yorkers are crazy about beets. We love beets in salads. We love borscht. The problem with beets is that they are a pain in the neck to cook. A messy pot and lid; a messy stove, what with the splattered, lurid, magenta juice; a messy sink; messy hands from peeling and slicing . . . As I knew from experience, French produce markets offered beets that had already been cooked—not just cooked but peeled and vacuum-packed, no refrigeration necessary, long shelf life, absolutely perfect beets from Lorraine, ready to cut into chunks or slices. In fact, I have never *not* seen in French produce markets these beets that have already been cooked and peeled, with a choice of conventional growing methods or certified organic. They are cheap as dirt. French lovers of food have their priorities straight. Beets are something they enjoy every day; a salad without beets is just not a proper salad. Beets with chopped scallions, a mustardy vinaigrette—our custom-

Elaine's Clear Vegetarian Borscht

Serves 6

Elaine is Mitchel's mom, and this is her summertime staple, so I guess it isn't surprising that Mitchel loves borscht. I couldn't figure out the discarding of the beets. Why not just leave them in there or mash or puree them? Mitchel says no; he says he likes this borscht thinner because it's "more refreshing." OK. Sounded wimpy, but this is a superb borscht, so obviously he's right.

But, Mitchel, heh-lo-o-o? Why can't these nice people use the single most ingenious item in our store—exclusively in our store, I might add—my cooked, peeled, vacuum-packed beets from Lorraine? They're perfect: all the nutrients are locked inside each beet; they're delicious; and moreover they eliminate the time, effort, and mess of cooking beets.

Apparently you have to start with raw beets to make Elaine's borscht. Ah, well, the bonus is that you can add the beet greens, which up the flavor and probably make the soup much healthier too. Bear this in mind as you're waiting (forever) for the beets to cook and cleaning up the mess that you wouldn't have had if you had used precooked French beets instead.

1. Place the sliced beets and their greens in a large stainless steel stockpot or another nonreactive stockpot and add the onion. Pour in water to cover the beets and onion by just about 1 inch (about 12 cups). Bring to a boil, then reduce the heat and simmer until the beets are tender, 30 to 35 minutes.
2. Strain the broth into a glass container or another nonporous (and, therefore, nonstaining) container, discarding all the solids. While the soup is still hot, stir in the lemon juice, sugar, and salt; adjust the seasonings to your taste. Cover the borscht with plastic wrap and chill it in the refrigerator for at least 3 hours.
3. To serve, ladle the soup into chilled bowls and drop a big dollop of sour cream into each serving. Or, if you want to be dramatic, serve it in glasses, also topped with sour cream.

2 bunches (about 2½ pounds) red beets with healthy beet greens, washed well, beets thinly sliced and greens reserved

1 medium Spanish onion, thinly sliced

½ cup fresh lemon juice, or to taste

½ cup granulated sugar, or to taste

2 tablespoons kosher or sea salt, or to taste

Sour cream, for serving

Chef's Note: You are aiming for a potent borscht starter, so take care not to add too much water when filling the pot—that would dilute the soup. If you decide you want to add more water later, you can.

I was on my way to spend a week working myself to exhaustion in Paris (a different restaurant every night of the week; grueling days hiking through SIAL, a biannual international food show). There I sat waiting for takeoff at Newark airport, working on my second stiff Bloody Mary. I had a dish of warm cashews at my right hand and was holding my hearing aid in my left hand, between my index finger and my thumb.

Remember the great book by Oliver Sacks, *The Man Who Mistook His Wife for a Hat*? What a book! Well, you can call me The Man Who Mistook His Hearing Aid for a Cashew.

I molar-crunched my state-of-the-art, $2,100 digital hearing aid into about sixteen pieces. We hadn't even left the ground, and I was stone-deaf. I had two backups, though, each of exponentially decreasing technology; and if I'd had a third, it would have been an ear trumpet like Grandpa's.

ers went nuts for them. They made the *New York Times,* too, with a color photo and exclusive attribution to Fairway. I was so proud. We sell mountains of them today, and, still, no other shop in the country has them. The only thing I miss, despite the $100 billion worth of them we have sold in the years since I first got them here, is not being able to eat the just-scalded tops of freshly cooked beets, the beet greens, with sea salt, while I wait for the bloody things to finish cooking. But I am getting over it.

Then I started bringing in dried beans (legumes, pulses) from France, though varieties grown not just in France but all over the world—*gros plats* (sort of like an ordinary cannellini bean, but bigger and flattish); flageolets, the great French beans from the southwest; the tiny *coco blanc* and *coco rose; pois chiches* (chickpeas or garbanzos, which Italians call *ceci*); *fèves* (fava beans); the great du Puy lentils from my cherished Auvergne region, arguably the most prolific cheese-producing region in the world. I even got unpopped popcorn, which was really not very good. What is novel about the beans is that they are packed in mesh sacks weighing just over 1 pound. Irresistible. The great cassoulet beans began to show up, too—Soissons, Castelnaudarys, and the rare and ridiculously expensive Tarbais beans. Pink lentils from Champagne and lentils from the Berry region, where almost all the greatest French goat's milk cheeses come from.

Later I found a company specializing in cooked, vacuum-packed vegetables and beans—potatoes three ways, tiny peeled ones whole or cut into slices or cubed; sliced carrots; cubed beets; leeks; red beans; white beans; flageolets; lentils; even ears of corn.

Around this same time, I learned that the best prune in the world comes from sprawling plum orchards around a wonderful town called Agen in the Lot-et-Garonne department in southwestern France (*département* in French corresponds to our word "county"). Agen is right on the Garonne River, the north side of which is considered regionally to be a part of Guienne, if not actually Gascony, of which Guienne was once part. In any case, the area is a paradise for the food lover. Gascony is known chiefly for foie gras, confits of duck or goose, and Armagnac, cognac's less famous cousin.

Pruneaux d'Agen are sweeter, tenderer, and prettier than California prunes, if indeed a prune can be considered pretty. The Agenais prune is a specific variety, the Ente, and the plum tree it grows on has gorgeous pink and purple flowers in the spring; as you can imagine, these flowers contribute mightily to the beauty of the area. Pruneaux d'Agen find their way into numerous recipes in Gascony cooking—in stews involving lamb or mutton; in stuffings; as an accompaniment to duck, goose, and chicken; for *confitures* (jams); and even for aperitifs and eaux-de-vie. I import them in bulk, and we sell tons, at a price much lower than even I can believe.

I also discovered that a little company that dries the Ente plums that become pruneaux d'Agen has perfected a method it calls "soft-drying." This company offers me figs and apricots that are tender, succulent, and visually stunning, unlike ordinary dried figs and apricots—not to mention that all of them are grown in the south of France rather than in California or Turkey. It is simply a fact that fruit from these old, small orchards is better-tasting than fruit from the massive commercial crops grown elsewhere.

Now we receive soft-dried strawberries, pineapple from Senegal, mango from Cameroon, Charentais and Cavaillon melons, little cubes of coconut meat from the coconut palms of the Ivory Coast. Soft-dried banana, also from plantations in the Ivory Coast, is a revelation. There's also a mix of three different varieties of raisins, huge, meaty, supersweet, moist, and fragrant, a complete revision of everything you

Roasted Leg of Lamb with Flageolet Beans

Serves 8 to 10

This is not a recipe you can make on the spur of the moment, but it's a special yet rustic meal, well worth the time. Leave plenty of simmering time for the beans—it can take 3 or 4 hours to get them truly, meltingly, tender.

LAMB:

1 whole leg of lamb, bone-in and oven-ready (about 8 pounds)

2 to 3 large garlic cloves, peeled and thinly sliced

2 tablespoons extra-virgin olive oil

2 teaspoons kosher or sea salt

1 teaspoon freshly ground black pepper

Leaves from 2 sprigs thyme

3 celery stalks, trimmed and roughly chopped

3 carrots, peeled and roughly chopped

1 medium Spanish onion, peeled and chopped

½ cup dry white wine

BEANS:

1 cup salt pork or slab bacon, rind trimmed, diced

Up to 3 tablespoons unsalted butter, as needed

½ cup diced carrot

½ cup diced Spanish onion

½ cup diced celery

2½ cups dried white flageolet beans (about 18 ounces, or 500 grams), soaked overnight in 8 cups cold water and drained

1. Using a sharp paring knife, cut small, shallow slits all over the leg of lamb and insert a garlic slice into each slit. Rub the leg of lamb all over with the oil. Next, rub it with the salt and pepper and sprinkle it with the thyme. Place it in a large roasting pan, cover it with plastic wrap, and let it marinate at room temperature while you prepare the beans.

2. In a large pot over low heat, cook the diced salt pork or slab bacon, stirring frequently, until crisp, about 40 minutes. Use a slotted spoon to transfer the bacon to a paper towel–lined plate to drain. Pour off all but 3 tablespoons of the accumulated fat (or add butter to the pan to make a total of 3 tablespoons if the pork didn't render enough fat). Add the diced carrot, onion, and celery and sauté until the vegetables start to brown, about 10 minutes.

3. Add the soaked, drained flageolet beans to the pot, along with the browned salt pork, the white wine, and enough chicken stock to cover the beans. Place the parsley and thyme sprigs, the peppercorns, the bay leaf, and the garlic clove on a large piece of cheesecloth and tie it closed with kitchen twine. Add this bouquet garni to the beans.

4. Raise the heat to medium-high and bring the beans to a simmer, stirring frequently. Cover the pot, reduce the heat, and simmer gently until the beans are tender (depending on the age of the dried beans, this could take up to 4 hours—older beans take longer to cook).

5. When the beans are mostly cooked and just slightly al dente, stir in the salt. Preheat the oven to 450°F.

6. When the oven is hot, place the lamb on a rack in the center position and roast for 30 minutes. Scatter the celery, carrot, and onion around the lamb; reduce the oven temperature to 375°F; and continue to roast for 1 hour and 15 minutes. At this point, the lamb should be beautifully browned and cooked to medium in the outer portions, with the doneness varying to rare closer to the bone (something for everyone). Remove the roast from the pan, transfer it to a carving board, and let it rest for 15 minutes uncovered before slicing.

7. Meanwhile, make gravy by placing the roasting pan on the stovetop (use two burners) over medium heat. Pour in the ½ cup white wine and simmer, stirring and scraping the vegetables and browned bits from the sides and bottom of the pan into the pan juices. Strain this liquid into a saucepan and cook for about 3 minutes over a medium flame to burn off the alcohol. Stir in ½ cup water and simmer for approximately 5 minutes more, stirring from time to time, until the gravy is reduced to ½ cup. Taste, season with salt and pepper if necessary, and transfer it to an insulated gravy boat or carafe to keep warm.

8. To serve, drain the cooked beans and mound them along one side of a warmed serving platter. Thinly slice the lamb by taking hold of the exposed bone with a clean dish towel and cutting horizontally with a sharp carving knife. Arrange the slices next to the beans. Drizzle the lamb with a little of the gravy and serve the rest in the gravy boat on the side.

2 cups dry white wine

2 to 3 cups All-Purpose Chicken Stock (see recipe, page 116) or low-sodium broth

2 sprigs flat-leaf parsley

2 sprigs thyme

8 peppercorns

1 bay leaf

1 garlic clove, peeled

2 teaspoons kosher or sea salt

Butcher's Note: No need to trim any fat from the leg of lamb before roasting—the fat will melt and baste the meat during the cooking, and once it's sliced diners can leave the rim of fat on their plates.

Christmas plum puddings are already here. Jan Buhrman (Kitchen Porch) on Martha's Vineyard has made them for us for the last three years. Cloth-wrapped, gorgeous, delicious, easily the best plum puddings since their invention in the Middle Ages. Back then, the word "plum" was used for any dried fruit—plums in the modern sense are curiously absent from plum puddings. "Plum" usually meant "raisin." Little Jack Horner stuck in his thumb and pulled out a raisin? In any case, Fairway has the old "limited supply" of bloody plum puddings. And no hard sauce. We ain't got no hard sauce.

ever thought about California raisins. These French people add no sugar to raisins, bananas, apricots, figs, or prunes. They do add cane sugar, just a bit, to peaches, pears, apples, strawberries, cranberries, pineapple, papaya, melon, and mango. I have long preached the gospel of serving these soft-dried fruits instead of fresh fruit with serious cheese and charcuterie.

I then began to import France's best onions. Onions are important. No vegetable is more crucial, not even garlic. I have found that onions are much more than onions, once you get involved with them. Our good old Spanish onion is perfectly fine, as are the purple or "red" onion and the white onion. Plus, we now have sweet varieties: the name-controlled Vidalia from Georgia, Maui Sweets from Hawaii, Walla Wallas from Washington State, and the Texas One-Oh-Something or other.

France and Italy have onions that have been famous for centuries, for very good reasons—firmness, heat, moisture, flavor, and fragrance. French onions from the Tarn valley and the foothills of the Pyrenees; the super-famous Roscoff onions from fields near the seacoast of Brittany; the spectacular, storied, sweet, purple-skinned Calabrian onion called the Tropea (after a village), which begs to be roasted or grilled, is also from fields near a coast, the Tyrrhenian coast of Italy—the part of the Mediterranean that laps up against Corsica, Sardinia, and the Italian mainland. The Tropea is very, very sweet, owing to the low sulfur content of the soil it grows in. It's also very, very red, and longish. Once you've sliced up a mess of Tropeas to combine with tomatoes and, say, avocado, cukes, or fresh herbs like lovage, basil, and chervil, you'll be absolutely delighted. Me? I'm absolutely thrilled. The onion,

A Rundown of American Onions

Spanish onions are the gold standard for American onions; the issue is whether you want the great big ones or the smaller ones. Buy whatever size is easier for you to handle. Vidalias and other sweet onions are for people who really don't like onions, I'd say. The low sulfur content of the soil they're grown in makes them sweet rather than onion-hot—to me, that's a different variety of vegetable. Red onions were called Bermuda onions where I came from. They are much hotter than Spanish onions, and I prefer to use them raw rather than for cooking. White onions are as hot as Spanish onions but are the choice of lots of professionals, who insist they're easier to chop. I don't think I agree, but there you have it. In all, there's nothing wrong with American onions.

even more than the potato, is the most important vegetable. And to say that these onions are the best in the world is to say a mouthful, because there are a lot of great onions in the world.

But the onion that engendered the most publicity for Fairway is the echalion, grown in Poitou, southwest of Paris. As its name implies, the echalion is more shallot (*échalote*, in French) than onion. What is endearing about it, aside from its wonderful flavor—sweet and shallotty—is that echalions are torpedo-shaped, so they can be cut or carved in ways neither an onion nor a shallot can be: medallions; long, straight slivers; hollowed-out canoes for stuffing. Echalions are useful cut into coins and used raw for salads, and they are grand roasted whole, along with beef and chicken, and in gratins and soups. We've imported them by the ton for years now, and I've yet to see them in any other market. They are beginning to show up on some restaurant menus, though, so someone besides Fairway must have gotten hip to them.

Soon after my discovery of the echalion came the venerated Brittany shallots, gray shallots from southwestern France, yellow shallots from the Massif Central (Auvergne). And not long after that, I went nuts for French garlic.

ven before I was first impressed by the garlic that grows in France and Spain (Italy's is surprisingly ordinary, unless I'm missing something), I didn't have much respect for Gilroy, California's, garlic. There's nothing particularly wrong with it at face value, but I knew that there had to be better, stronger, longer-lived, prettier garlic. Sure, pretty is as pretty does, but Gilroy ain't so pretty, and it ain't doing much, either. Now, that statement may be heresy. I've been to Gilroy, and I've been to the yearly garlic festival there, where garlic ice cream is served and garlic toothpaste is sold. I do feel like a heretic saying anything negative about California's garlic industry, much as I feel about saying anything negative about its almond industry, its olive and olive oil industry, its boring strawberries, and its soporific Monterey Jack cheese, the cheese for people who don't really like cheese.

I learned about *ail Rose de l'Autrec,* the famous, name-controlled pink garlic of southwest France. Its growing season is short, and so is its availability: the demand for it is such that it's gone by Christmas, and it comes on the market only in late August. It's gorgeous stuff, sold loose by the head or braided into kilos and half kilos, and it keeps well. You name a French chef, and I'll guarantee you he or she uses *Rose de l'Autrec,* or maybe the purple Cadours from nearby, as purple a purple as the pink garlic is pink. Not the inner cloves themselves, just the outer parchment. This is garlic so powerful you are driven to roast whole heads of it, one or two to the diner (and these heads are at least half again bigger than any head of Gilroy garlic I ever saw), as an accompanying vegetable to make a lusty meal lustier.

The Cadours garlic growers offer braided purple garlic that has been smoked. This is an ancient tradition: braids of garlic were stored in the chimney for lack of anyplace else to put them, and they would, of course, be perfumed by the hardwood smoke. This garlic gave its smoky soul to everything it was added to. Toulousiennes became inured to it, and the practice survives today in the cassoulets and soups and stews of this glorious food region.

Two more of my famous imports are sauerkraut and walnuts. My sauerkraut comes from Alsace, where *choucroute* is more than cured, shredded

Pasta with Roasted Garlic

Serves 4

This is Mitchel's simple, elegant variation on a Pugliese classic. The better your garlic, the better this dish will be. I'd use our terrific Cadours or *Rose de l'Autrec.* Or forget about the pasta and serve the roasted garlic heads as a first course. Toast or heat some good bread and mash up a crock of crème fraîche with a middle-aged goat's milk cheese like chabichou du Poitou. When you press the garlic cloves with your fork, a molten, custardy mousse of garlic will ooze out. Make little open-faced sandwiches out of the chèvre spread, the garlic, and the bread. I like a Rhône red with it, if not a bourbon or Scotch on the rocks.

3 garlic heads (yes, heads)

½ cup plus 2 tablespoons extra-virgin olive oil

1 pound dry pasta (I like angel hair; my Italian wife thinks pasta has no business going finer than spaghettini)

Kosher or sea salt

Freshly ground black pepper, to taste

6 to 8 fresh basil leaves, cut into thin ribbons

Freshly grated Parmesan cheese, to taste

1. Preheat the oven to 400°F. Peel away some of the papery outer layers from the garlic heads, leaving the skins of the individual cloves intact. Using a sharp knife, slice about ½ inch off the top of each head, exposing the cloves. Place the trimmed heads in a small roasting dish and drizzle 2 tablespoons of the olive oil over them, using your fingers to coat the heads evenly with the oil. Bake until the cloves feel very soft, about 1 hour. Let them cool just enough so you can handle them easily, then use a paring knife to slit the skin of each clove and pull the softened garlic from its jacket. Mash roughly with a fork, and then cover to keep warm. (At this point, as Steve has suggested, you could stop, pour a glass of wine, cut a few slices of some good bread, and as my mother-in-law would say, "go to town." However, let's exhibit a bit of self-control and proceed with the recipe.)

2. Bring 6 quarts of water to a rolling boil and throw in 1 tablespoon of salt. Add the pasta and cook to al dente (firm to the bite).

3. Meanwhile, in a large pan over low heat, heat the remaining ½ cup of olive oil until warmed through. Stir in the mashed garlic cloves.

4. Drain the pasta very thoroughly and add it to the pan with the warm olive oil and garlic, tossing over low heat to coat. Season generously with salt and freshly ground black pepper. Sprinkle with the basil and Parmesan and serve immediately.

Chef's Note: Garlic is sharp and aggressive only when raw. (As a matter of fact, the smaller you chop raw garlic, the stronger it gets.) Roasting it in its skin brings out the rich nutty flavor and mellows the bite.

Variation: As an alternative to roasting, you can poach peeled garlic cloves in olive oil. Please resist the urge to use store-bought pre-peeled garlic, which is dried out and bereft of flavor. The best way to peel garlic is to lay the flat of a chef's knife over the clove on a cutting board and smash it down with the palm of your hand. The skin will come off easily. Put the peeled cloves in a small ovenproof dish (a baking ramekin would be perfect) and cover with olive oil. Cover the pan with foil and bake on a rimmed cookie sheet (in case the dish bubbles over) in a 375°F oven for about 45 minutes, until the cloves are soft. You can also use the garlic oil you've created when you assemble the pasta dish.

cabbage; it is also the name of the dish, the recipe, for which it is made, *choucroute garnie,* in which wursts and ham, roast pork, and pieces of roast duck and goose are intermingled with caraway or aniseed, juniper berries, potatoes, and white wine. This sauerkraut is aged in wooden barrels for a full year, with riesling and fatback (*saindoux*), and is decanted into twenty-five-kilo tubs. This stuff is a far cry from the sour, mushy, characterless condiment found in supermarkets and at hot dog pushcarts. *Choucroute d'Alsace* is served throughout France, not just in *choucroute garnie,* but as a worthy companion to seafood and poultry as well as other meats and vegetables not even remotely related to Alsace or western Germany.

The walnuts of the Périgord region of France, just above the Lot-et-Garonne, are as revelatory as anything I have ever come across. California walnuts are perfectly fine, but Périgord walnuts are better, astonishingly delicious. I have spent a lot of time in Périgord, for its goat's milk cheeses, its walnut oil, and its foie gras. There is no place in the world I would rather be. It is so pretty there it hurts. And with Bordeaux so close by, even the meanest restaurant or café will have a wine list that is a wonder. The famous caves of Lascaux, near Brive-la-Gaillard, have been closed to the public since 1963, in order to protect the mind-boggling prehistoric wall sketches of red cows, yellow horses, bulls, black stags, and the bird-headed man. You can visit the caves; you just can't go into them. As I recall, they were discovered by four teenage boys in 1940.

Périgord walnuts are sent to me two ways: shelled—just the perfect nutmeat in vacuum-packed sleeves weighing 500 grams (just over 1 pound)—and as whole walnuts in red mesh sacks, also weighing 500 grams. Inside each package is a label that tells the world these walnuts are name-controlled, or AOC. I love to serve the whole walnuts with cheeses and charcuterie. Extracting the meat from the lovely shells using nutcrackers and picks is a pleasurable, tactile thing to do at table. I highly recommend it.

It's one thing to stock superb fruits and vegetables, every day, 365 days a year, particularly since many people think the name of our store is Fairway Fruits and Vegetables. But it's another thing to take this to a higher level. I suppose the highest level would be if all the farmers in the sixteen closest states raised and harvested perfect seasonal produce, loaded up their harvests, and made a beeline for us. But that's unrealistic. We'd be continually out of stock on 90 percent of the entire category, and we can't run a market like that. So we have no choice but to succumb to the reality of a global agribusiness through which thousands of supermarkets across the country have easy access to tomatoes in winter and asparagus in summer. Stone fruit comes to us all winter from Chile. Almost decent winter tomatoes come from Israel. Literally everything that grows and is edible—except for items such as fresh white and black truffles, porcini (*cèpes*) mushrooms, and fresh figs, each of which is still subject to seasonality—is part of the business of global horticulture, and it all hurtles seemingly effortlessly through the pipeline to us. Admittedly, seasonality is of primary importance to the serious chef, but the serious chef has to be realistic, too. During the brutal northeastern winter, the unrealistic serious chefs would be limited to root vegetables, shallots, and potatoes. That's just not going to happen. They have restaurants to run.

But in my traipsing around Europe, it occurred to me that Europeans have ready access to a lot of wonderful produce of a rarefied quality that we don't get here. Some of it is legal for import. We are forbidden by the USDA to import most tomatoes from Europe, for example, because of insects in the soil, fruit flies, or whatever. The USDA is understandably chary of the havoc an infestation could provoke. But the Netherlands, Belgium, and Israel have a special dispensation from the law, a "relaxment," whereby certain growers of hothouse tomatoes have been enjoying huge success in the United States. We can't bring in citrus fruits, either—as with tomatoes, there's a fear of nonindigenous insects. But Spain (the region of Valencia, principally) has a relaxment that has given us the irresistible clementine, a winter citrus fruit whose absence is unimaginable. My boss Harold was instrumental in pioneering the import of the wondrous clementine.

So I was burning to bring in some fruits and vegetables from France, Italy, and Spain. I found wooden punnets of potatoes grown in Lorraine. A punnet is a wooden container about as big as a shoe box—it holds 1 kilo (2.2 pounds). These were little potatoes: *rattes, francines,* and *reine charlottes.* The *ratte* is *the* potato to serve with raclette, the raw cow's milk cheese made either in the Swiss canton of Valais or in Savoie or Franche-Comté, just across the French border. *Raclette* comes from the French verb *racler,* "to scrape." This is why: the wheel of cheese, weighing 14 pounds or so, is split in half, and its face melted, either by placing it on bricks on a hearth very close to the fire or by fastening the cheese to the swiveling arm of a modern raclette machine, common in restaurants and homes in France and Switzerland. When the cheese is molten, the arm is swung away from the electric heating element or the half wheel is hoisted away from the hearth and a layer of melting cheese is scraped onto your plate. This is accompanied by boiled potatoes (ideally, *rattes*), boiled onions, cornichons, and crusty bread. Well, I wanted this potato, and I wanted it in those marvelous punnets.

And I got it. I didn't even have to fly the *rattes* in; they went on a container ship with a bunch of my other stuff. Sold the absolute hell out of them, and of subsequent shipments, for something like two months. I got them in the *New York Times* food section with Florence Fabricant's solo attribution to Fairway and a color photo. People were coming from out-of-state to get their hands on them, until our erstwhile next-door "competitor" ratted us out to the USDA. It turns out you're not allowed to import potatoes. Our government, whether out of a fear of infestation or as a means of protecting the powerful Idaho potato industry, is strict about this. No spuds. I should have known that, but I didn't. Well, you can have the ones from Prince Edward Island (PEI) in eastern Canada. But not from France. PEI potatoes are nothing to write home about, though far be it from me to criticize a potato, no matter how pedestrian it may be.

That wasn't the only lesson I've learned the hard way—it wasn't even the hardest lesson I've learned. An incident that occurred about eight years ago taught me this valuable rule: "Ask questions. Never assume." My closest Italian food colleague is Luigi ("Gigi") Sidoni. Gigi's exporting company, which is based in Milan, supplies us with a lot of Italian staples, delicacies, and rarities. The artisanal rarities I serendipitously stumble over in my travels must be trucked from distant villages all over Italy and Sardinia and Sicily to Gigi's warehouse, where they can be

Rustic Potato-Leek Soup with Optional Lardons

Serves 5

No need to tell me your mouth is watering right now, because I know it is. I worship potatoes, and there is no vegetable I enjoy—crave—more than leeks. And anytime I get to sprinkle a hearty handful of crisp, bacony *lardons* on something, I'm there.

1. In a large, heavy soup pot, melt the butter over low heat. Add the leeks, carrots, celery, and a pinch of salt and cook, stirring frequently so the vegetables don't brown, until softened, about 15 minutes.
2. Add the chicken stock, raise the heat to high, and bring the soup to a boil. Reduce the heat and simmer gently for 25 minutes. Add the potatoes and simmer until they are cooked through, 15 to 20 minutes.
3. Meanwhile, if you're making the *lardons,* spread the bacon in a large, preferably nonstick skillet. Cook over medium-low heat, stirring occasionally, until the bacon is crisp and well browned, 10 to 15 minutes. Use a slotted spoon to transfer the *lardons* to a paper towel–lined plate to drain.
4. When the soup is ready, season it with salt and white pepper. Ladle it into bowls and garnish with the parsley, and the *lardons* if you are using them.

4 tablespoons unsalted butter

3 leeks, well cleaned (see Chef's Note), all but 1 inch of the greens trimmed, very thinly sliced

2 medium carrots, unpeeled, scrubbed and cut into ¼-inch dice

1 celery stalk, cut into ¼-inch dice

Kosher salt

2 quarts all-purpose chicken stock, preferably homemade (see recipe, page 116)

2 large Idaho potatoes, scrubbed but not peeled, cut into ½-inch dice

½ pound slab bacon, rind trimmed away, cut into sticks ¼ inch square by ¾ inch long (for the *lardons*—optional but delicious!)

Freshly ground white pepper, to taste

4 sprigs flat-leaf parsley, roughly chopped

Chef's Note: Don't forget to take pains getting the grit out of those leeks. Split them down the middle and wash, wash, wash under the cold tap.

Tuscan White Bean Soup
with Escarole and Fennel Sausage

Serves 6

This fine soup really hits the spot. I like to serve it—just as we always serve my wife Michelle's minestrone—with a thick slice of bread placed in each bowl before the soup is ladled on. Then we drizzle some olive oil into it, and then sprinkle on some grated Parmesan. The oil doesn't have to be Tuscan, but I do suggest an oil that is big and robust, as most Tuscans are. Whatever you do, don't substitute squishy canned beans for the dried ones called for here.

3 quarts all-purpose chicken stock, preferably homemade (see recipe, page 116)

One 8-ounce can crushed plum tomatoes

¼ pound dried white beans, soaked in cold water overnight and drained

1 large carrot, peeled and diced

1 large celery stalk, trimmed and diced

1 large Spanish onion, peeled and diced

½ pound hot fennel sausage, casing removed, crumbled

1 large bunch escarole (about 10 ounces), roughly chopped

Kosher or sea salt and ground white pepper, to taste

Olive oil, grated Parmesan cheese, and crusty bread, for serving

1. Bring the chicken stock to a simmer in a large soup pot. Add the tomatoes, soaked beans, carrot, celery, and onion. Bring to a boil, then reduce the heat and simmer gently until the beans are completely tender, 1½ to 2½ hours.

2. Meanwhile, heat a large, heavy skillet over medium-high heat and add the sausage. Cook the sausage, using a wooden spoon to break it up, until well browned, 10 to 15 minutes. Use a slotted spoon to transfer it to a paper towel–lined plate to drain.

3. Stir the sausage and escarole into the soup and cook for another 10 minutes. Season with salt and white pepper. Ladle into bowls, drizzle with olive oil, and pass the Parmesan cheese and bread at the table.

Grocer's Note: Any dried bean will shine here. If you can get Tuscan *borlotti,* do try them, but cannellini, great northerns, or whatever you've already got will be just fine.

palletized, loaded into containers, and trucked to the port at Genoa, where container ships set sail for Port Elizabeth, New Jersey, and ultimately Fairway.

Gigi calls one day and says I simply must let his friend, the owner of a very big Italian produce supplier, put together a few pallets of seasonal this, that, and the other thing (it was early June, a great time for seasonal Italian fruits and vegetables), and send it to me by air freight. Gigi says this guy sends produce all over the world from Italy and knows what he is doing. I respond, yeah, he knows what he's doing in Europe, but does he know anything about clearing customs and FDA and USDA exams in the United States? Gigi assures me that his friend will assume all responsibility and that I will have no problems. With that, I proceeded to allow this guy to pallet up and fly to me a number of cases of what proved to be the most glorious, gorgeous fruits and vegetables I have ever been or will ever be a party to.

But none of it—save a solitary wooden crate of Calabrian garlic— was legal. The uniformed, gun-toting FDA official who was permanently ensconced at the Alitalia freight hangar at JFK jumped all over the stuff before my customs broker had even seen the documents and before the USDA officials even knew it had arrived. I shot out to the airport early that afternoon, and was given documents that had been stamped REFUSED in big red letters on every page. OK, I thought. Refused. Darn. What a shame. But Gigi said this wasn't my responsibility and it wouldn't cost Fairway anything. Could I at least look at the stuff to see what I was going to be missing? Sure. Right over there. Right over there was about half a mile across the gargantuan airplane freight hangar. I found a jumbled pile of tossed cases of fruits and vegetables shrouded in the netting used to bind the pallets onboard the jet. What have we here? Hmmmm.

There were wooden crates of the most beautiful artichokes I had ever seen—*castraure*, the wildly anticipated spring artichokes grown in the Veneto, below Venice; they're "castrated" in that they are rogue side-shoot thistles from below the main choke, so tender and sweet that they are usually eaten raw, sliced thin, choke and all, and served with just lemon juice and olive oil and a few shavings of Parmigiano.

There were wooden crates filled with *ciliegine bianchi,* the famous Italian white cherries, bursting with juice, that grow in Emilia-Romagna and other places in Italy.

There were wild arugula and *puntarelle,* both coveted salad greens, and *radicchio di Treviso,* the stiletto-shaped reddish-purple chicory, *"cuore di toro"* (bull's heart) tomatoes, and lemons from Sicily.

But those artichokes . . .

So. Thanks for the hospitality, I say to the woman from the FDA. What a shame, eh? I can have that case of garlic? Great. Thanks again. I'll be off.

Commence lesson to be learned the hard way.

"Na-na-na-na," she intones. "Where do you think you're going? You're not finished with this. You can't just walk away. Well, you can. But then I'll be fining you to the tune of three times the value of this entire shipment. Plus, your company will be red-flagged on every customs entry list in the country, *and* with every FDA and USDA entry list, too." This meant that every time something I was importing arrived at a seaport or an airport, every bell, whistle, and siren within a five-mile radius would go off.

I had to go to another location not too far away from JFK, a decrepit building housing the only licensed fumigator the USDA authorized to do his dirty work on the entire East Coast. I had to buy forms, one for each case of produce on that shipment, at a cost of $2.75 apiece. I then had to fill out and sign every single form. There were 485 crates, boxes, and cases of produce on that shipment. It took a couple of hours. It was now midafternoon. I had to be at the French consulate in Manhattan, on Fifth Avenue, at five PM. I was being elevated to *prud'homme* status, the highest level of the Guilde des Fromagers, the French brotherhood of *maître fromagers* (master cheesemongers). So I rushed back to the Alitalia freight hangar. I would just make it to the consulate once I was able to drop off the "fumigate and destroy" forms with the FDA's representative. I found her at her desk, in a windowless, dimly lit, terribly depressing cubicle that served as her office. I dutifully and obsequiously thanked her, proffered the forms, and figured I was already history to her. She informed me that now I was required to load every case of produce onto my truck under her squinting, unrelenting, unamused scrutiny, and, accompanied by her, transport the stuff to a nearby Dempsey Dumpster, at which point she would stand idly by, arms akimbo, while I tossed every single case into the Dumpster.

"I'm not going to require that you fumigate this time. It all looks clean." (If it's clean, why don't you just let me drive away with it?) I thought it. I didn't say it.

All that meant was I didn't have to take the stuff back to the derelict fumigation building, have it fumigated overnight at an enormous cost to Fairway, and then return to the airport for the fruits and vegetables toss.

Now, in New York, early June means 107 degrees—at least it did that day. So there I was in the back of a truck, tossing crate after crate from the truck into the maw of a Dumpster and sweating like a Singapore stevedore.

No wide-ribboned, intricate medallion went around my neck that afternoon. No Frenchman kissed me on both cheeks. I missed that ceremony by a country mile.

Layered Provençal Vegetables

Here is a signature recipe of Mitchel's, a dish he has been offering for years. He and Carmela used to call it a *bayadère,* referring to the striped costume of the eponymous Indian temple dancer in Marius Petipa's ballet *La Bayadère,* first performed in Saint Petersburg in 1877. But I never quite felt that the word suited the dish, and Mitchel is oblivious to all sorts of real knowledge—he really couldn't care less what the word means. That bothered me, and I wouldn't stop nagging him about it, until he eventually stopped calling it a *bayadère.* Thank goodness he didn't stop making the dish, which is as delicious as it is lovely. It's a colorful side that accompanies roasted meats very well.

2 pounds thinly sliced Spanish onions

5 tablespoons extra-virgin olive oil

1½ teaspoons kosher or sea salt

Freshly ground pepper, to taste

1 pound thinly sliced zucchini

1 pound thinly sliced yellow squash

1 pound thinly sliced plum tomatoes

1 pound thinly sliced small eggplant (the diameter of the eggplant should be similar to that of the other vegetables—Japanese eggplant works well here)

6 to 10 whole garlic cloves, smashed (skin left on)

6 sprigs thyme

1. Preheat the oven to 475°F.
2. In a large skillet, sauté the onions in 2 tablespoons of the olive oil over low heat until very brown and caramelized, 45 minutes to 1 hour. Spread the onions in the bottom of a 9-by-13-inch roasting pan. Season them with ¼ teaspoon of the salt and pepper to taste.
3. Layer the raw sliced vegetables on top of the onions in upright standing rows: one row of zucchini, one row of yellow squash, one row of plum tomatoes, and one row of eggplant. Repeat, if necessary, until the pan is full and very tightly packed (the vegetables will shrink a little as they roast). Season with the remaining 1¼ teaspoons salt and with more pepper; drizzle with the remaining 3 tablespoons of oil. Tuck the smashed garlic cloves and sprigs of fresh thyme in among the vegetables. Roast until tender and browned to your liking, 1 to 1½ hours. Serve immediately.

Chef's Note: The longer these vegetables roast, the more delicious they become, but the color is more vibrant with a shorter roasting time. Chef's choice!

Plum tomatoes on the stand at one of the stores.

Epilogue

I come from a place so unlike my beloved New York that I can hardly believe it. Thirty-two years I've lived here (can't believe that either), but in some ways I'm still the same kid as ever—I still hate it when summer winds down. I guess I can understand why. Most of my childhood memories of summer have to do with food. My mom is an amazing cook, and so was my grandmother. Surely the groundwork they laid is responsible for the person I am today.

One long-ago summer food that immediately comes to mind—and my mouth waters at the mere recollection—is wilted lettuce salad. When I was a kid in Columbia, Missouri, everybody had a garden. My mom, born and raised in western Kentucky, would combine just-picked lettuce—still warm, living, and breathing—with sliced onions, also from the garden, and not much else. It was the dressing that took the dish over the top. Bacon grease with sugar and red wine vinegar poured hot over the Bibb, butter, or green leaf lettuce (or all three), tossed, and served right away.

(Now that I think of it, how could I not have grown up to become addicted to balsamic vinegar?)

So many summertime foods helped to shape my personality. Sorghum poured over vanilla ice cream. All-you-can-eat fried clams at the Howard Johnson's out on the highway. Root beer so cold you can't drink it for a few minutes, in heavy glass mugs sitting on a tray attached to your car's rolled-down window at the Mugs Up out across the rickety bridge over Hinkson Creek. Mom's corn fritters straight out of the pan served with maple syrup. Mom's fried sweetbreads. I had no idea what they were, but I loved them. To this day, espying them on menus, I never fail to order them. Mom's Yorkshire pudding, served only with prime rib, which we referred to as roast beef, and her remarkable gravy. Mom's oyster dressing in roast turkey. Oysters and Yorkshire pudding in Missouri? Go figure.

We didn't have much in the way of exotic foods, but I still managed to cultivate some interesting tastes. Yucatan gum, sort of like Teaberry gum but better, was always in the top drawer of Nana's dining room cupboard. And serious licorice, lozenge-shaped like your big thumb; and horehound. Popcorn balls, a joy. What made these extraordinary was that the plain old Jolly Time white popcorn was popped in bacon grease (always), then rolled into snowball-size balls held together with sugar and butter. And we would make our own taffy—you had to pull it and pull it. A trip to the pharmacist at the D&H drugstore to cop vials of pure cinnamon oil in order to soak toothpicks to suck on in school. They were so hot our eyes would stream, but as we sucked, the toothpick became milder and pulpy and you could masticate it, still powerfully infused with cinnamon oil. And there were those little bundles of sassafras bound with string, sold at Safeway on Broadway for little old ladies to make tea. We would suck on the sticks, rectangles about three inches by three-quarters of an inch, and chew on them until our tongues were like leather.

And there was riding our bikes—this is hardly food, but it's an undeniable olfactory celebration: riding behind the mosquito fogger contraption attached to the back of a jeep. Doubtless a carcinogenic fog, it was so thick we couldn't see to steer our bikes. It was almost as good as riding behind a Greyhound bus. The exhaust was like perfume.

But back to those summertime flavors of yore that still inspire me: homemade peach or strawberry ice cream. Local peaches, local strawberries, natch. My granddad's tomatoes, lettuce, asparagus, sweet peppers, hot chiles, huge green onions, and kohlrabi. My grandmother Nana and I would pull kohlrabi out of the ground, wash the dirt off with a hose, devour the crisp, peppery things standing right there in the garden. And there were the Jonathan apples down at McBaine near the Missouri River. They were stored in dark barns filled with hay, dust, and the aroma of cider and apples. There was a lady apple tree in Nana's front yard facing the beautiful Parkway, with that sparkling, crawdad-teeming creek tinkling down the center. We used to push those apples onto sharp sticks Nana would clip from the tree. You could whip a springy stick, laden with a lady apple, back; sling it forward; and launch the apple on an arcing journey, so high and so far you thought you were Superman, clear across the creek. I caught and kept crawdads from that creek as pets; I never ate them. I had no concept of eating them, more's the pity. Same with the tadpoles, but I don't rue that omission.

All that fantastic food, all that local produce—decades before buying local became fashionable. It's probably no surprise that as an adult I wasn't satisfied with what I found at the supermarket, that I went in search of something better, even broadened my search overseas. You probably have similar memories. Mine them to develop your own tastes.

And then go farther. I want you to study maps of France, Italy, Spain, all the countries around the Mediterranean, all the islands in it. Read all the best books about food. Among my favorites are *Honey from a Weed* by Patience Gray, *The Auberge of the Flowering Hearth* by Roy Andries de Groot, and *When French Women Cook* by Madeleine Kamman. Read Waverly Root's *The Food of France*, *The Food of Italy*, and just plain *Food*. Read everything by M. F. K. Fisher, Elizabeth David, Patricia Wells, George Lang. Read the food-related writings of A. J. Liebling and Joseph Wechsberg (and their other brilliant work too). You can't go wrong with Jacques Pépin's cookbooks—and if you see that he's on television, drop whatever it is you're doing and watch; he's the best there is.

Stop spending so much time and money in restaurants, and instead entertain at home. I want you eating at your own table. I don't care if it's you doing the cooking, as long as someone is. Don't fall for food fads, because the old ways are best—the old tools, the old recipes. The more somebody messes with a foodstuff, refines and improves it, the less good it's going to be. And don't cut stuff out of your diet—eat everything, but eat it moderately. Get some exercise, then eat like a hero and push yourself away from the table before you overdo it.

Buy the very best you can find and afford. If there is no Fairway near you, you're simply going to have to cajole, needle, badger, and cultivate your grocer into at least striving for something higher. Tell him what you want him to carry. Persist. If his olive oil selection is lame, let him know about it. If he tells you he can't find the stuff you want, have him contact me.

Don't get all exercised about organic food—it's often not as good as food produced conventionally. Often, conventional is as organic as a product can be; it just hasn't been certified for various reasons, usually the cost of certification. Yes, do strive to use and eat local food, but let's not get ridiculous. And, if you really want to eat local, cultivate and tend a vegetable garden of your own.

Remember that what you're eating today, how you're eating it, is creating food memories. Like my own memories of those marvelous childhood summers, they will sustain and inspire you and those you love for years to come.

$2.49 LB

POMEGRANATE
$3.49 EACH

Produce FAIRWAY
BOSC PEARS
1.99 LB

List of Recipes